Ancient Indian Economic Thought

Ancient Indian Economic Thought

Relevance for Today

Ratan Lal Basu
Raj Kumar Sen

RAWAT PUBLICATIONS
Jaipur • New Delhi • Bangalore • Mumbai • Hyderabad • Guwahati

ISBN 81-316-0125-0

Published by
Prem Rawat for **Rawat Publications**
Satyam Apts, Sector 3, Jawahar Nagar, Jaipur 302 004 (India)
Phone: 0141 265 1748 / 7006 Fax: 0141 265 1748
E-mail: info@rawatbooks.com
Website: www.rawatbooks.com

New Delhi Office
4858/24, Ansari Road, Daryaganj, New Delhi 110 002
Phone: 011 2326 3290

Also at Bangalore, Mumbai, Hyderabad and Guwahati

Typeset by Rawat Computers, Jaipur
Printed at Chaman Enterprises, New Delhi

Contents

1

Introduction

Ancient Indian Economic Thought

In the conventional academic circles, we trace the origin of accounting, banking, commodity production and all other laws and concepts of economics and commerce in Britain especially, to the British Industrial Revolution of the late eighteenth century. Roots of these ideas are traced in the works of Adam Smith and his predecessors in the West (Panchamukhi, 2000: 1).

There are innumerable well-written books and articles on thoughts of Adam Smith, Mercantilists, Physiocrats, and various other western economic schools. As regards ancient economic ideas, the convention economists refer to Greek ideas, even to the Old Testament. Unfortunately, very little effort has been made to explore the economic ideas inherent in the vast body of ancient Indian literature. Western education has generated a feeling of disdain for ancient Indian culture and tradition among a large number of intellectuals. On the other hand, another school of thought expresses the view that there was everything of modern knowledge in ancient Indian writings. From these two biased views it is very important to filter out the essential aspects of ancient Indian achievements in different branches of knowledge and study whether they are relevant in the current age or not.

Anyone showing interest in ancient Indian economic ideas is likely to come up against insurmountable barriers since one class of intellectuals holds the view that it is a sheer fantasy to conceive of the existence of analytical economic ideas in ancient Indian Sanskrit literature. Others opine that it is all divine and beyond the scope of scientific study. Bias, either way, is equally troublesome as regards unraveling the truth inherent in ancient Indian texts. It is necessary to avoid both these prejudices and adopt a scientific and bias-free approach while trying to look for economic ideas relevant for modern problems in ancient Indian texts.

Many scholars, particularly during the high-tide of nationalist movement in the first half of the twentieth century, attempted to make an objective and unbiased evaluation of ancient Indian economic ideas explicitly or implicitly contained in ancient Indian writings, particularly in Vedas, Arthaśāstra, Rāmāyaṇa and Mahābhārata, Manusmṛti, Śukranīti and other ancient texts. The objective observation of M.A. Buch is worth noting in this connection. He opines that economic ideas are but reflections of actual economic conditions of society. In ancient India, there had been considerable development of trade, commodity production and cash economy. So, economic ideas naturally developed in order to provide guidelines to traders, manufacturers and the rulers to perform their respective duties in a harmonious way (Buch, 1979). Another noteworthy aspect of ancient texts was that they were by no means rigid or static. They were revised and rewritten from time to time in accordance with the changing economic and socio-political conditions. This is the reason why there are so many Arthaśāstras and Dharmaśāstras. Many of the Dharmaśāstras are still extant; among the Arthaśāstras proper, only that of Kauṭilya has so far been discovered, but others have been mentioned several times by Kauṭilya and many other ancient Indian authors. This dynamism of ancient Indian texts makes them qualitatively different and valuable for future generations as they are amenable to modifications in conformity with changing objective conditions. However, we cannot expect to find the economic ideas associated with modern industrial economics in ancient Indian writings as there is no evidence of the existence of modern factory industries and industrial capitalism in those days. In this study our purpose of research in ancient Indian economic thought is not to try out any ancient model in unmodified form (as happened in case of copying blindly the western models after independence) for the Indian economy today. We however believe that study of ancient Indian economic ideas is likely to endow us with a deeper insight into our culture and tradition and the inherent national characteristics. This is all the more so because long foreign domination (for about a millennium) and indiscriminate experiments, with imported foreign models especially after political independence, have generated much confusion. In fact, it is impossible to find the appropriate model for economic development of our country, nor to diagnose the real causes of failures of models tried so far, unless we have a clear idea about the inherent characteristics of our nation, which have been distorted beyond recognition over the last millennium or so.

In this connection, it would not be out of place to have a glimpse of the Chinese experience. Policies of modern mainland China have always been framed with due consideration of their traditions extending over thousands of years into the past. This is true for both Maoist and post-Maoist policies. If we are attracted by the recent Chinese success, we should first recognize this fact. Similarly, the Japanese, after the Meiji restoration, framed development policies by paying due regard to their national heritage and cultural tradition. Their spectacular success, during the post Second World War period, owes considerably to this practice of converting western models according to requirements of Japanese culture and tradition.

These are important lessons from two most economically powerful nations of Asia. In spite of this fact, a significant segment of Indian intellectuals opt for western models in unmodified form and rejoice in disparaging our culture and tradition. One reason for this may be the lack of objective research into ancient Indian texts. However, the good news is that as a reaction to the dogmatic views of westernized intellectuals (of both the capitalist and the socialist camps) disparaging Hindu culture and tradition, there has emerged a school holding the diametrically opposite view that revival of ancient Indian ideas and methods will solve all our problems and we have nothing to learn from modern western civilization. Unfortunately, both the opposing camps have built up their views on sheer dogmas, sometimes even without an iota of knowledge of ancient Indian texts. Thus it is high time to have an objective study of ancient Indian traditions and their modern relevance since without such a study, we cannot come to any definite conclusion regarding the suitability of ancient Indian traditions to solve our current economic problems.

In this regard, Aiyangar observes: "…the historical interpretation of old systems of social thought, such as may result from a comparative study with their analogues, may help us to realize how social institutions have to be adjusted to the needs of the times, and how systems of thought have to be interpreted in connection with their peculiar purposes. The old Indian literature to which by analogy the Cameral designation has been suggested may still be of value. Let us consider its skilful adaptation of means to ends, its logical deduction of rules of conduct from its socio-religious hypothesis, and its attempt to combine ethical, political and economic purposes in individual and social action. The attempt to view their teachings in their natural perspective and to interpret them in relation to our times as well as theirs might help in the dawn of the brighter day which we all wait and hope" (Aiyangar, 1949: 175-76).

Notwithstanding the difference in political systems, many guidelines as delineated in ancient Indian texts are still relevant. If properly adapted and implemented, they may streamline the functioning of the various economic policies of the government today and remove many hurdles in the path of successful implementation of these policies. In many cases the guidelines in the texts were purely normative and indicated the ideal policies. Some of these are more realistic for the modern era considering the communication revolution and computer facilities available today. Many ideal tasks which were impossible to accomplish in those days have become quite easy to accomplish in the computer age. For example, price control, as delineated in Arthaśāstra, was really an arduous task in those days, but today it appear to be very simple with the assistance of computers, even if the number of commodities involved are million times more than that of those days.

There are, however, various obstacles in the path of unraveling the truth inherent in ancient Indian literature. Unlike the study of western literature, it is not at all easy to dig out clear-cut and uncontroversial ideas from the vast body of ancient Indian literature. The Greeks were well known for historical writings. This tradition was carried on in the west during the Roman and subsequent periods. The history of ancient China has also been well documented by historical and religious authors of that country. Unfortunately, we do not have any such coherent record of ancient Indian history and traditions. Many important ancient Indian texts have been totally lost or irreparably damaged because of negligence, and many of them had been deliberately destroyed by barbaric invaders.

Informations regarding ancient Indian history and traditions are scattered in the Vedas, Puraṇas, the Epics (Rāmāyaṇa and Mahābhārata), the Dharmaśāstras, the Jātakas, and the Arthaśāstra of Kauṭilya (no other proper Arthaśāstra has yet been discovered). Excavations and rock inscriptions are other sources of information. Greek authors like Scylax (c. 509 B.C.), Hecataeus, Herodotus, Ctesias, Photius, Nearchus, Strabo, Onesicritus, Diogenes, Kleitarchus, and Megasthenes (fragments of his Indika survive in the works of Strabo, Arrian, Diodorus and Plinius) provide valuable information about ancient Indian history and traditions. But it is very difficult to piece together the fragments of information obtained from diverse sources and construct a coherent economic history of ancient India.

In spite of these problems, painstaking study and research are likely to bring out many valuable information regarding ancient Indian economy and economic policies. Such research is likely to have very limited success in unraveling the truth inherent in ancient Indian texts that is relevant for modern India. Nevertheless, it is likely to pave the way for further research in this area. With this purpose in view we will concentrate in this study on two major ancient texts, viz., Manusmṛti, and the Arthaśāstra of Kauṭilya.

Among the Dharmaśāstras the text known as Manusmṛti occupies a very important place because of its wide coverage and detailed guidelines for various aspects of human living.

To quote: "Many myths have since very early times clustered round the name of Manu. He is regarded as perfect in study of the Veda, in the knowledge of its meaning, and the performance of its precepts. His origin is said to be divine and he is sometimes declared to be even a manifestation or incarnation of the Supreme Soul. ...Different Vedic works belonging to different Schools declare, 'All that Manu said is medicine, i.e., salutary.' He is said to be the fountain head of all the Smṛtis or traditional lore and Bṛhaspati, while proclaiming the superiority of Manu on the score of his strict adherence to the Veda, clearly declared that a text opposed to Manu is not commendable. ...The *Paṇḍits* adhere to the above view up to the present time. This supreme position of the author justly commanded the unflinching adherence of the Hindus and made the work exceptionally popular. The completeness of the work, its intelligibility and its orderly arrangement also contributed to the same result" (Sen, 1976: xii-xiii). On the basis of evidence from ancient Indian texts the author of the present Manusmṛti flourished at least before 3000 B.C. (*ibid.* Introduction, p. xvi). The original Manusmṛti was written and revised several times later on to take account of the current problems of different ages. The original Manava Dharmaśāstra is likely to be different from the work which now goes by the name of Manu. It is clear from the fact that some of the *ślokas*, attributed to Manu by Vaśiṣṭha and others, are not to be found in the present text (*ibid.:* ix).

According to some authors, "The Manusmṛti had probably attained its present form by the 2nd century A.D. …We find that though the Smṛtis had begun at an early date and were supposed to have been based upon Vedic injunctions and customs, yet new Smṛti authorities sprang up giving new injunctions which can hardly be traced to Vedic authorities. Many of the older authorities were again revised to harmonize the changes made and these revised editions passed off as the old ones as there was no critical apparatus of research for distinguishing the new from the old" (Dasgupta and Dey, 1962: xxvi).

There are also many *Vāṣyas* (commentaries) on Manusmṛti. The most popular available *Vāṣyas* are of Medhâtithi, Kullûka Bhatta, Govindarāja, Sarvajña-Nārāyaṇa, Rāghavānanda, Nandana, Rāmachandra and Gañgādhara. They reflect the transition in the methods for interpreting the text in accordance with the changes in values with changes in time.

Before 1905, historians and scholars interested in ancient India did not have access to any reliable manuscript of Kauṭilya's Arthaśāstra. But references of this book were found in other available ancient Sanskrit literature, e.g., 'Nītisara' of Kamandaka, 'Daśa Kumara Charita' of Daṇḍīn etc. (Shamaśāstry, 1967: vii-xii). The existence of a manuscript of Kauṭilya's Arthaśāstra came to light in 1902 by Shamaśāstry, the then librarian of Oriental Manuscripts Library of Mysore, when it was handed over to the library by a *Paṇḍit* of Tanjore district. Shamaśāstry produced tentative English translations of the text in *Indian Antiquary* in 1905 and in the following years. The full text was edited and published by Shamaśāstry in 1909 (*ibid.:* v). Comparing this text with citations and references in other ancient works, scholars and experts on ancient Indian literature agreed that Shamaśāstry's edition was really the copy of the work composed by Kauṭilya (Majumdar, 1960: 140), though the existing text is perhaps not absolutely word for word that which was written by Kauṭilya. It is apprehended that many sections of the original work have been lost and there might be some interpolations by authors belonging to later generations (*ibid.*: ix; also Sastrī, 1967: 200). Nevertheless the available text is a rich and reliable source of research on Kautilya's economic and other ideas.

Our present study is based on the available texts of Manusmṛti and Kauṭilya's Arthaśāstra and their English translations. In Chapter 1 we look into the essence of the ancient Indian tradition and world outlook as embodied in various *sāśtras*, i.e., ancient Indian texts, and compare them with the western world outlook. Indian traditional viewpoint conceives of a balance between baser and eccentric aspects of human nature (necessary for our *saguṇa* material existence as distinct from the *nirguṇa* supreme self) on the one hand, and the nobler and concentric elements on the other. The mainstream western world outlook on the other hand, is based on the trade-off between material aspects and spiritual aspects of human living. So far as material achievements in the West according to the capitalistic view prevailing there is concerned, the baser aspects (*artha* and *kāma*) are the sole guiding forces. This approach has resulted in the ruthless exploitation, untold human sufferings, and wanton destruction of ecology and environment in course of material progress in the West. This approach cannot provide the right guidelines for framing policies for economic and social development in India. So, we must look into ancient Indian literature to seek the right path for India's economic development. In this book, we have concentrated on two ancient Indian texts, viz., Manusmṛti and Kauṭilya's Arthaśāstra, to search for proper guidelines.

In Chapter 2 we deal with the relevance of Kauṭilya's agricultural policy for revitalizing the agricultural sector in modern India. As the majority of the population of India is still dependent on agriculture for their livelihoods, it is an urgent necessity to step up agricultural production without any long-term adverse consequences on soil and ecology. It had been expected that the introduction of HYV (High Yielding Varieties) technology would pave the path for long term sustainable development of Indian agriculture, but a few decades of experience with the new technology has resulted in widespread disillusionment. In spite of the apparent success of the new agricultural technology, it has led to long-term adverse consequences like pollution of soil and underground water by chemical fertilizers and pesticides; serious ecological hazards like arsenic pollution; and loss of natural seed varieties suitable for various climatic conditions and having the natural capability to resist the attacks of pests and diseases. India has already lost most of its natural seed varieties by indiscriminately copying the western practice of using hybrid seeds, which lack the natural capability to resist the vagaries of climate and attack of germs and pests. So, we believe that Arthaśāstra guidelines may be of considerable help in solving various problems of Indian agriculture today in spite of differences in many respects between the age of Kauṭilya and that of present India. Since Manusmṛti has very little to say so far as agriculture is concerned, so in this chapter we concentrate on the guidelines and prescriptions as found in Kauṭilya's Arthaśāstra.

In Chapter 3 we have taken up the environmental issue. In recent years, awareness about environment and ecology arose only since the middle of the twentieth century. In fact, the current wave of environment awareness got a fillip only after the United Nations Conference on Human Environment held in 1972 at Stockholm (Sweden). The matter gained further importance after the Earth Summit held in 1992 at Rio de Janeiro (Brazil). But long ago, in ancient Indian texts, we find awareness pertaining to the preservation of environment and ecology of the planet Earth. One major shortcoming of recent measures, both at the national and at the international level, is that they are mainly *ad-hoc* in nature and lack holistic approach. In fact, these measures are designed to solve specific problems and do not spring from any basic cosmological and holistic view. So, it has become difficult to coordinate and harmonize various types of activities and agencies designed to protect environment and ecology. These approaches may solve some specific problems pertaining to environment and ecology but would fail to remove the basic cause which leads to the generation of damage to environment and ecology. This cause lies in our world outlook and view regarding nature and our relationship with it. In this regard we may learn from the two ancient Indian texts discussed in this book. For example, Manu specifies (In *ślokas* 1/27 to 1/57) why we should think of ourselves as a part of the harmonious universe and therefore regulate our material activities in accordance with the rules of nature. This approach towards environment and ecology is likely to generate deeper awareness about these matters among the common people so that they will be more willing to spontaneously cooperate in eco-preserving drives of the government or the NGOs. Kauṭilya's detailed specifications point out how every measure towards preservation of ecology and environment are coherently integrated.

It is true that environmental and ecological problems today are more severe and complicated than those at the time of Manu and Kauṭilya. Many aspects of environmental problems were totally absent in those days. But, if we look deeply into the matter we will realize that all man-made environmental and ecological problems arise because of our greed or ignorance that makes us commit things contrary to the balance of nature. The root cause of ecological problems is this and therefore it is the same for all ages.

Thus, we see that the ancient texts may not only help us in solving specific ecological and environmental problems, but also they may give us deeper insight into the matter, which will help us to solve our problems in a more harmonious way.

In Chapter 4 we have considered the relevance of the ancient policy for revival of craft industries as a safety net after New Economic Policy (NEP) was implemented in India. In course of industrialization, particularly during the era of liberalization, one of the most serious problems facing India is the problem of increasing unemployment, as modern industries are highly capital intensive. It is an urgent necessity to find a safety net for job seekers. The handicraft industries are likely to play a major role in this regard, but this sector is burdened with various problems, most of which have remained unresolved in spite of efforts by the Government of India since the First Five-Year Plan.

In ancient India, these craft industries were highly developed and efficient. So, the question arises whether we can learn from the ancient texts as regards reviving the craft industries and making them capable of creating enough jobs.

The most mention-worthy thing in this regard is that job creation through the crafts automatically takes place if the crafts prosper without any subsidy or government reservation, which is an undesirable aspect of the present policy regarding crafts in India. In ancient India this was possible because of the high quality of products of the crafts. In this regard also, Manusmṛti does not provide any detailed information. So, in this chapter, also, we consider mainly the guidelines provided by Kauṭilya's Arthaśāstra.

Nowadays, many cheap goods are produced by the large-scale modern industries, but there are also craft products, which depend on human skill and therefore cannot be imitated by modern industries. These products are likely to command a large market only if the quality of products is ensured. But, it is here that the craft industries in India today fail. Because of the low quality of products the craft industries require government reservation. Their substandard products cannot be sold unless the government departments buy them or they gain monopoly power through government reservation. This policy of generating employment through the crafts is definitely at the cost of the consumers and, therefore this is not at all desirable. In this chapter we will study how the quality of products was ensured in ancient India. This was mainly done by the guilds and strict government regulations on them regarding quality of products of the craft industries.

In Chapter 5 we have discussed the necessity of the state sector even in the era of globalization for which we can take lessons from ancient texts. We can identify many areas where direct state participation is not only justified but also essential even in the era of liberalization. But these sectors must be identified properly and operated efficiently with least possible corruption. The basic problems of the state sector in India today are inefficiency and widespread corruption. Manusmṛti hardly attaches any importance to the state sector. But in the Arthaśāstra we get a vivid description of the state sector and prescriptions for operation of this sector in a socially desirable and sustainable manner. Here we may take lessons from the Arthaśāstra, which specifies in detail how state sector activities could be run efficiently and with least possible corruption. The coherent approach towards discipline and accounting, punishment for violation of rules and negligence of assigned duties, punitive measures for corrupt officials etc., as prescribed in the Arthaśāstra, are likely to be of considerable help to make the state initiative run efficiently, in the selected areas, with least possible corruption. This is the lesson from and relevance of the Arthaśāstra for India today.

Price policy is the subject matter of Chapter 6. Both Manusmṛti and the Arthaśāstra provide clear guidelines for controlling prices in a socially desirable manner so that the producers and the traders can earn reasonable profit and at the same time the consumers are not deprived of their right to buy goods at affordable and reasonable prices. There are also specific guidelines, especially in the Arthaśāstra, as regards handling situations of excess demand or excess supply in a desirable manner.

It is likely that emulation of the basic features of these policies would convert our ill-administered price policy under planning into a well-administered one, which would be capable of restoring balance in the market mechanism, facilitating unhindered functioning of the market mechanism, and bringing about welfare of the majority of the population of the country. It is desirable that prices of most of the commodities are determined by the forces of the market. But prices of some sensitive commodities should be fixed and directly regulated by the state. At present the list of commodities for administered pricing are haphazardly selected, often at the behest of the vested interest groups. This is not at all desirable. The question is one of selecting the appropriate commodities for which prices should be administered by the state.

In Chapter 7 we have pointed out the shortcomings of tax and fiscal policy in modern India and suggested how ancient policies could help overcome these shortcomings. Nowadays, many countries have gone into heavy fiscal and budgetary deficits covered by borrowing (both internal and external) and deficit financing (circulation of new paper notes) for facilitating economic development. But if these deficits do not result in increase in investment and production, deficits are incurred to finance mainly the consumption expenditure of the state, and unproductive and wasteful expenditure cannot be controlled, this will lead to serious problems for the economy. In fact, this is the bitter experience of India in recent years. A substantial part of new borrowing (both internal and external) is required for the repayment of old debt along with interest. So at this stage lessons from the ancient Indian texts, especially, Manusmṛti and Arthaśāstra, may be of much help for maintaining a sound finance.

Chapter 8 deals with financial security and property rights of women, which were ensured by *Strīdhana*. One of the most important issues for which ancient Indian literature has much relevance today is women's rights and empowerment. Nowadays, there is much discussion about this issue. Even an International Women's Year and Decade were observed. In India various showbiz measures for empowerment of women have been adopted since independence, e.g., reservation for women in various jobs, legislative bodies etc. There are also legal measures against oppression of married women in the husband's family. But still there are no specific measures to ensure financial security of women, without which all other measures are likely to become meaningless. Financial security of women was given top priority in Manusmṛti and Arthaśāstra of Kauṭilya. Particularly, the concept of *Strīdhana* (woman's property) gives us an idea how financial security of married women till her dying day could be ensured. In fact, one undesirable aspect of western culture on our society in recent years is the inducement to disintegrate the family system, which is the building block of Indian society. So the culture ensuring permanency of marriage is to be encouraged to obviate the harmful influence of nihilistic western culture. In this respect assurance of women's financial security is an urgent necessity. The ancient concept of woman's property, if revived in a modified form to suit the needs of modern society, is likely to play an important role in ensuring women's financial security. This is the most mention-worthy relevance of ancient texts as regards empowerment of women.

In Chapter 9 we look into the question of division of labour. The essence of the prescriptions in this regard in ancient texts is that professions should be chosen on the basis of aptitudes of persons. Once properly chosen, one should stick to the profession selected and should receive perfect training. In this respect, we cannot deny the role of heredity in selection of professions. Since heredity in many cases attributes some inherited qualities from the very birth, and training facilities are also the best if one selects his profession by this criterion. In fact, in many cases professions are chosen in this way even today. But this cannot be a hard and fast rule in the modern world. A person who has no aptitude for his father's profession, but is competent for some other profession, ought to get the opportunity to adopt that profession.

But there should be a proper method of screening the aptitude of a person and also systems of rigorous and appropriate theoretical and practical training for each person entering a particular profession. There should also be rigid restrictions on frequent change of professions. These are the relevant guidelines we may adopt from the essence of the prescriptions of the ancient texts as regards division of labour. Both Manusmṛti and the Arthaśāstra give us basic guidelines of division of labour in a proper manner. In this context however, we must remember that the ancient caste based division of labour may not be perfectly suitable for modern Indian society. So, it may be necessary to modify the guidelines provided in Manusmṛti and the Arthaśāstra to suit the objective conditions of modern India.

Chapter 10 deals with the issues relevant for good rulers. Corruption and dishonesty of politicians have become important issues in recent years. In fact, Indian democratic system has almost become meaningless because of the unethical lifestyles of politicians of all ranks. So to all patriotic and honest citizens of the country, it is of utmost necessity to investigate the basic cause of this horrible situation and to devise some way out. It is also of utmost necessity at present to devise some means to make the politicians free from corruption. Guidelines in Manusmṛti and the Arthaśāstra may be of considerable help in this regard. Although those measures had been devised for making a good king under monarchy, but they can be modified to select and train political leaders in democratic India today.

In Chapter 11, we go into the issue of globalization. Early Indian history reveals India's trade relations with not only Asian countries and Greece, but also with African and European nations. But we should remember that although 'globalization' in the sense of free-trade existed in India since the pre-historic time, it was not exactly the process of 'globalization' according to modern terminology. In fact, globalization, as the term signifies in recent times, implies free movement of capital from one country to another without any restrictions. This also indicates freedom of industrial houses owned by foreign nationals to establish branches in any country. These things were completely absent in ancient times. Still we may have some guidelines regarding globalization from ancient Indian texts. Manusmṛti, by denigrating global connections, has indirectly pointed out the dangers of globalization with foreign domination. Kauṭilya is liberal as regards globalization, but he clearly points out that all international economic transactions should serve the interest of the nation in the first place. The basic lesson from these texts regarding globalization is that we should welcome globalization, but after preserving our sovereignty and freedom (economic, political, strategic, social and cultural). The most important matter in this context is related to inter-country free-movement of capital. The most crucial among the conditions, imposed by the world bodies on all countries undergoing structural reforms and globalization, is the provision for free inflow of foreign capital. At the same time there is hardly any provision for free international mobility of labour.

Endnote

It is very difficult to incorporate in a small book all aspects of the ancient Indian tradition contained in the vast ocean of ancient Sanskrit literature. This is a preliminary study but we expect to open up the path for further and deeper research into the topics covered by us and also on those that we have not covered. Our endeavour would be meaningful if our tiny effort induces scholars to go into deeper research into the treasure of ancient Indian literature.

This monograph owes a good deal to Motilal Bhimraj Charity Trust, Delhi, especially its Managing Trustee Dr. Bharat Jhunjhunwala, who took the initiative in sponsoring a seminar during October 27-28, 2004, at Rishikesh, inviting comments from eminent scholars on ancient India from various parts of

India on our initial manuscript. The two day discussion with valuable comments from Swami Shanti Dharmananda, Dr. Bharat Jhunjhunwala, Dr. S.D. Chamola, Dr. M.G. Basavraja, Prof. Uday Jain, Miss B.R. Shanta Kumari, and Prof. R.K. Jha enriched our insight into ancient India, and enabled us to modify and improve the quality of our manuscript on the basis of their comments, criticisms and suggestions. The following invitees who could not attend the seminar, also helped us in the same way by mailing their comments: K.K. Somani, G.C. Bhattacharya, Prof. Shashi Tiwari, Dr. V.K. Hampiholi, Paramananda Mittal, Swami Muktananda Saraswati, K.D. Gangrade, A. Dange and Dr. Smrti Kumar Sarkar. We express our heartfelt thanks and gratitude to all of them.

Although the monograph is authored by us, the virtual architect of this book is Dr. Bharat Jhunjhunwala, the Managing Trustee of the Motilal Bhimraj Charity Trust, Delhi. In fact, it was Dr. Jhunjhunwala who gave us the idea that it was high time to write such a book. Since then, at every stage of our research relevant to this book, we received unconditional assistance from him including liberal financial grants from his trust. We once again express our gratitude to Dr. Jhunjhunwala and all other eminent scholars who provided us with invaluable suggestions.

The following scholars also provided us with many useful suggestions and comments in various stages of preparing this book: Dr. Pratap Chandra Chunder (translator of Arthaśāstra in English), Rosita Dellios (Bond University, Australia), Late Maggie Grey (Bond University, Australia), Lawson Smith (Central Queensland University, Australia), and Satyabrata Narayan Chatterjee (Bhairab Ganguly College, Kolkata). We are also indebted to the Oriental Research Institute, University of Mysore, for organizing and inviting us to the International Symposium on Kauṭilya's Arthashastra, held at Mysore during June 13-16, 2002; to Dr. Dhanapat Agarwal, Director, Swadeshi Research Institute, Kolkata, for inviting us to various seminars on

Indian Tradition organized by the said Institute in collaboration with Merchant Chamber of Commerce. We express our gratitude to the employees of the publisher and printing press. We also express our thanks to the 'progressive' intellectuals, politicians and authors who rejoice in disparaging our cultural heritage, and to those who directly requested us to refrain from writing a book on ancient India, as according to them, those thoughts have become completely obsolete and can by no means have any relevance for modern India. In fact, vehement opposition and sarcastic comments from them strengthened our determination to give a fitting reply by completing the work.

References

Aiyangar, K.V. Rangaswami (1949): *Indian Cameralism, a Survey of Some Aspects* of *Arthaśāstra*, The Adyar Library, Madras.

Buch, M.A. (1979): *Economic Life in Ancient India*, R.S. Publishing House, Allahabad.

Dasgupta, S.N. and Dey, S.K. (eds.) (1962): *A History of Sanskrit Literature*, Vol. I, University of Calcutta.

Majumdar, R.C. (1960): *Ancient India*, Motilal Banarasidass, Delhi.

Panchamukhi, V.R. (2000): *Indian Classical Thoughts on Economic Development and Management*, Bookwell Publications, New Delhi.

Sastri, K.A. Nilakanta (ed.) (1967): *Age of the Nandas and Mauryas*, Motilal Banarasidass, Delhi.

Sen, S.N. (1976): *Manusmṛti*, Chapter VII (English translation), Vidyodaya Series No.16, Chattopadhyaya Brothers, Calcutta.

Shamaśāstry, R. (ed.) (1967): *Kauṭilya's Arthaśāstra*, Mysore Printing and Publishing House, Mysore.

2

Sources and Essence of Ancient Indian Tradition

Contrast between Mainstream Western World Outlook and Ancient Indian World Outlook

The objective of this study is to spell out various aspects of traditional economic concepts as conceived in ancient Indian literature, which are relevant for certain specific economic problems of India.

In fact, ancient Indian economic concepts are inexorably associated with ancient Indian way of life. The vast body of ancient Indian literature spelling out various aspects of traditional way of life may be categorized in the following manner.

At the central point of ancient Indian world outlook lie the four Vedas: Ṛgveda, Sāmveda, Yajurveda and Atharvaveda.

From these Vedas spring four Upa-Vedas:

(i) Āyurveda from Ṛgveda
(ii) Gāndharvaveda from Sāmveda
(iii) Dhanurveda from Yajurveda
(iv) Arthaśāstra from Atharvaveda

Next to be mentioned are the Dharmasūtras in the form of Sūtras (short prose).

Thereafter, we have six *Aṅgas* (*Sarāṅgas*): Yotis, Vyakarana, Chhanda etc.

Next in order come Smṛtis or Dharmaśāstras written mainly in *ślokas*.

Then are the six major Philosophies:

1. Vedānta of Bādarāyana
2. Nyāya of Gautama
3. Mīmāṃsā of Jaiminī
4. Yoga of Pātanjali
5. Sâṃkha of Kapila
6. Vaiśeśika of Kaṇāda (Swāmī Śantī Dharamānanda Saraswatī, 2000).

These six philosophies differ in the outer mode of presentation, but all of them essentially converge to one central point, the Vedic world outlook – the question of balance between two sides of the four *Puruṣārthas*, viz., *dharma*, *artha*, *kāma* and *mōkṣa* – *dharma* and *mōkṣa* belonging to the nobler side and, *artha* and *kāma* to the baser (but essential for material existence) side.

We may mention next the Upaniṣadas, Bhāgavad Gītā, 18 Purāṇas, four Upa-Purāṇas and the Epics (Vyāsdeva's Mahābhārata and Valmikī's Rāmāyaṇa).

As our present study is based on a Dharmaśāstra (Manusmṛti) and an Arthaśāstra (of Kauṭilya), we will deal with these literary forms in more detail as given below.

Dharmaśāstras

They are written in *śloka* form and contain teachings on Hindu civil and criminal laws. The major Dharmaśāstra authors mentioned in ancient Indian literature are:

Añgira, Āpastamba, Atri, Dakṣma, Gautama, Hārita, Kātyāyana, Kusāna, Manu, Parāśara, SamVarta, Bṛhaspati, Vyāsa, Yājñavalka, Visṇu, Śatatapa, Śaňkha, Likhita, Vasiṣṭha, Yāma.

Vṛddha Gautama mentioned the names of 50 Dharmaśāstra teachers (including minor *smṛti* writers). If the references in commentaries are taken into account, the number is close to 100 (Sen, 1976: vii).

Most of these texts had been revised and rewritten several times and the revised versions of some of these texts with a large number of *vāṣyas* (commentaries) of each are still available (Dasgupta and Dey, 1962: ix).

Arthaśāstras

The Arthaśāstras are mainly concerned with the science of state-craft, but the political concepts in them are inextricably associated with economic, social and all other aspects of human living. Kauṭilya mentions the names of a large number of Arthaśāstra authors preceding him, like Bāhudantiputra, Bharadvāja, Dīrghacārāyana, Ghotakhamukha, Kaniñka Bharadvāja, Kātyāyana, Kaunapadanta, Kiñjalka, Parāśara, Piśuna, Piśunaputra, Vātavyādhi, Viśālākṣa (Chunder, 1995: 22-23).

Out of the texts written by these authors, Kauṭilya's Arthaśāstra has special relevance for the present study. It contains various aspects of political and economic principles in a detailed and comprehensive manner. In essence, Kauṭilya's Arthaśāstra (like all other *śāstras*), while delineating economic and political principles, sticks, on the whole, to the basic Indian world outlook.

It is, however, very difficult to specify the ages of the above-mentioned *śāstras*. On the basis of the studies of a class of historians, especially the Western school, it may be presumed that almost all of them (at least their original versions, which were re-written several times later on) had been composed between 1000 B.C. and 200 B.C. But, the historians with Indian world outlook hold that they are of much earlier origin, although they admit that they were rewritten several times according to the needs of the changing time and objective conditions of the country.

The *śāstras* were the outcome of the gigantic all-round intellectual efforts by a number of exceptionally competent post-Vedic Brahmin scholars who endeavoured to touch upon all conceivable aspects of human living in this material world and beyond, and to elaborate them in terms of the Vedic world outlook. These efforts resulted in the accumulation of a vast body of knowledge. Out of these sources, all branches of *śāstras* and philosophies developed in course of time. Chapter 59, Verses 29-74 of the *Śāntiparvam* of the Mahābhārata mentions the original source in the following mythical manner: "To start with, men were pious although they did not have any king or the rod of punishment. But in course of time they were afflicted with greed and other vices. This perturbed the gods who appealed to the creator, *Brahmadeva*, for devising some means to bring men back to the path of virtue. In response, the creator wrote a comprehensive manual with 100,000 chapters for man's guidance."

The book dealt with all aspects of human living, e.g., the *trivarga* of *dharma*, *artha* and *kāma* and emphasized four distinct subjects of studies, viz., *Trayī* (Vedic triad), *Ānvīkṣikī* (rational philosophy), *Vārtā* (economics) and *Daṇḍanīti* (law of punishment or coercion). This all comprehensive bulky book of *Brahmā* (the creator) was abridged by Śaṃkara into the *Vaiśālākṣa* (*Śāstra*) with 10,000 chapters; Indra, the king of the gods, into *Bāhudantaka* (*Śāstra*) with 5,000; Bṛhaspati, the chief priest of the gods, into the *Bārhaspatya* (*Śāstra*) with 3,000; *Kāvya* (or *Uśanasa*), the chief priest of the demons, into the *Auśanasa* (*Śāstra*) with 1,000 chapters (Kangle, 1986).

Now, we describe in brief the essence of ancient Indian traditional world outlook.

Essence of Ancient Indian Traditional World Outlook

The basic thread that interconnected all aspects of human living, according to ancient Indian world outlook, originated from the four Vedas and proliferated in all the *śāstras* of ancient India. This is the 'concentric' world outlook, conforming to the inner harmony and order of Nature.

Balance and Inner Harmony

Indian traditional viewpoint conceives of a balance between baser and eccentric aspects of human nature (necessary for our *saguṇa* material existence as distinct from the *nirguṇa* Supreme Self) on the one hand, and the nobler and concentric elements on the other.

Since independence, however, Indian economic policies have been designed on the Western world outlook rather than on the Indian traditional viewpoint. The adoption of the New Economic Policy (NEP, based on Liberalization, Privatization and Globalization) since 1991 further reinforced this trend. The basis of these policies is mostly the neo-classical economic theories, which have turned out to be the mainstream of thinking in the West. These theories have subdued all other viewpoints so far as material progress in the West is concerned. In the neo-classical school of thinking technical aspects of economic development have been overemphasized, shelving aside ethical and humanitarian aspects. This leads to imbalance as regards material progress since it overemphasizes the baser aspects (*artha* and *kāma*) and sidetracks the nobler ones (*dharma* and *mōkṣa*). On the other hand, Indian traditional world outlook conceives of a balance between material aspects (*artha* and *kāma*) and ethical-spiritual aspects (*dharma* and *mōkṣa*) of human living. Thus, the Western models, based on material progress alone, have been misfit for India. Before coming to any definite conclusion, however, we must properly diagnose the causes of the maladies Indian society is inflicted with, examine how far Western paradigms are responsible for these maladies, and how far the Indian traditional model is likely to provide any way out. For this we need to distinguish between the imbalance in the Western viewpoints and the inner balance of the Indian traditional world outlook.

Imbalance in Western World Outlook

This Western-style imbalance may be clearly defined as the trade-off between material aspects and spiritual aspects of human living. So far as material achievements in the West are concerned, the baser aspects (*artha* and *kāma*) are the sole guiding forces. There is no place for ethics or spiritualistic undertone. This approach has resulted in the ruthless exploitation, untold human sufferings, and wanton destruction of ecology and environment in the course of material progress there.

Now, let us look into the spiritualism of the West. The dominant spiritual practices in the West are based on Christianity. Christian ethics emphasizes on spiritual and ethical aspects of human living. To quote from *The Bible*:

> "Do not store up riches for yourselves here on earth, where moths and rust destroy, and robbers break in and steal. Instead, store up riches for yourselves in heaven, where moths and rust cannot destroy, and robbers cannot break in and steal. For your

heart will be where your riches are" (*The Bible*, *New Testament*, *Matthew-6* (*Luke* 12.33-34/19-21).

"No one can be a slave of two masters; he will hate one and love the other; he will be loyal to one and despise the other. You cannot serve both God and money."

"This is why I tell you not to be worried about the food and drink you need in order to stay alive, or about clothe for your body. After all, isn't life worth more than food? And isn't the body worth more than clothes? Look at the birds: they do not sow seeds, gather a harvest and put it in barns; yet your Father in heaven takes care of them! Aren't you worth much more than birds?"

"So do not start worrying: 'Where will my food come from? Or my drink? Or my clothes?' These are the things the pagans are always concerned about. Your Father in heaven knows that you need all these things. Instead, be concerned above everything else with the Kingdom of God and what he requires of you, and he will provide you with all these other things" *(ibid. Luke* 16.13; 12.22-31/24-33).

"Jesus looked straight at him with love and said, 'You need only one thing. Go and sell all you have and give the money to the poor, and you will have riches in heaven; then come and follow me.' When the man heard this, gloom spread over his face, and he went away sad, because he was very rich.

Jesus looked round at his disciples and said to them, 'How hard it will be for rich people to enter the Kingdom of God!'

The disciples were shocked at these words, but Jesus went on to say, 'My children, how hard it is to enter the Kingdom of God! It is much harder for a rich person to enter the Kingdom of God than for a camel to go through the eye of a needle" (*ibid. Mark*-10, *Matt.* 19.16-30; *Luke* 18.18-30/21-25).

The quotations clearly put forward the Christian ethics regarding accumulation of wealth. This principle goes against the mainstream capitalistic world outlook in the West that advocates limitless accumulation of wealth. In fact, many other philosophers and thinkers in the West endeavoured to propagate the gospel of ethics, but all their views were swept away in course of material progress.

So far as economic viewpoints are concerned, many humanitarian approaches were put forward by the Classical School of Western economists like Adam Smith, Ricardo etc; the Historical School; and the socialist thinkers like Karl Marx. But, the mainstream economics in the West gradually deviated from the humanitarian path. Since the emergence of the neo-classical economic theories, positive economics rather than welfare economics got the priority, and ethical aspects became irrelevant.

To quote:

> "Another surprising feature is the contrast between the self-consciously 'non-ethical' character of modern economics largely as an offshoot of ethics. Not only was the so-called 'father of modern economics', Adam Smith, a Professor of Moral Philosophy at the University of Glasgow (admittedly, a rather pragmatic town), but the subject of economics was for a long time seen as something like a branch of ethics. …
>
> "I turn to the other origin of economics – related to the 'engineering' approach. This approach is characterized by being concerned with primarily logistic issues rather than with ultimate ends and such questions as what may foster 'the good of man' or 'how should one live'. The ends are taken as fairly straightforwardly given, and the objective of the exercise is to find the appropriate means to serve them" (Sen, 1999: 2).

From the above quotations it is clear how the mainstream modern economic theories have rejected the ethical and humanistic aspects and concentrated on the 'engineering' aspect which concentrates mainly on the way efficiency in production could be achieved. In fact, here lies the basic philosophy of the capitalistic production from its very beginning.

The consequences of this approach towards material progress have been vividly put forward by Adam Smith. To quote:

> "It is this which first prompted them to cultivate the ground, to build houses, to found cities and commonwealths, and to invest and improve all the sciences and arts which ennoble and embellish human life, which have entirely changed the whole face of the globe, have turned the rude forests of nature into agreeable and fertile plains, and made the trackless and barren ocean a new fund of subsistence and the great high road of communication to the different nations of the earth" but "......is the cause of all the tumult and bustle, all the rapine and injustice which avarice and ambition have introduced into this world" (Smith, 1977: 24).

Capitalistic system opens up vast possibilities of betterment of the conditions of the traders and manufacturers, but in their reckless drive towards achieving higher and higher material gains, all ethical sentiments, fellow feeling and human values are bound to be swept away unless restrained by some outside force.

The branch of economics known as 'Welfare Economics', endeavours to deal with the normative aspect of economics, and ethical and humanitarian issues are likely to come up in course of considerations of welfare of the individual and social welfare. But the modern western 'Welfare Economics' is dominated by the concept of Pareto efficiency or Pareto optimality. According to Pareto criterion of efficiency, any change that makes at least one individual better off without making any other individual worse off is an improvement in social welfare. If any change makes everybody in the society better off, social welfare will definitely increase. Social welfare will decrease on the other hand, if a change makes no individual better off but makes at least one individual worse off. On the basis of this criterion modern Western welfare economics defines the state of maximum social welfare and economic efficiency. According to this definition, an efficient allocation of resources is such that it is not possible, by any reallocation, to make any individual better off without making any other individual worse off.

The Pareto criterion of efficiency claims that it is scientific and objective as it is completely free from any value judgments.

But, in fact, it is not so. To say that "a policy change, which makes some persons better off without others being worse, leads to higher social welfare" is itself a value judgment. This is because we recommend such changes which conform to the Pareto criterion. The implication of the assertion becomes obvious when the persons who gain as a result of policy change are the rich and those who remain in the same condition are the poor. According to the Pareto criterion, any change that improves the condition of the rich keeping the poor at the same state, increases social welfare. But this view is not likely to be accepted by the majority.

Secondly, the Pareto criterion fails to judge the desirability of those social changes which benefits some (say the poor majority) at the cost of others (say the well-to-do minority). Thus the policies related to removal of mass poverty or income inequality may not be permissible according to the Pareto criterion.

Moreover, the Pareto criterion leads to indeterminacy. To explain this let us start with a given situation where out of ten individuals the first individual receives all the income and the rest nil. If the total income is given, any income transfer to the remaining nine with zero income would aversely affect the first individual. So, this change is not permissible according to the Pareto criterion and the initial situation is one of Pareto efficiency. Again, if the initial situation is such that the first individual receives zero income and the total income is divided among the remaining nine, then this is also a Pareto efficient situation of income distribution, because any redistribution will adversely affect at least one individual. In fact, an infinite number of Pareto efficient income distribution is possible here (Graaff, 1957). The Pareto criterion has been used to justify the outcomes of the capitalistic production mechanism with all the maladies associated with it, like mass poverty, income inequality, unemployment, environmental degradation etc.

Now, let us have a glimpse of the psychosis of capitalistic production system. The basis of material advancement under capitalism is the animal spirit of the capitalists, viz., their uncontrolled greed. Karl Marx has aptly defined this mechanism by a simple format:

M-C-M', where M is the initial money capital of the capitalist who purchases inputs (C) with this money, converts them to final goods, and sells these goods to receive higher amount of money (M'). The difference between M and M' generates profit, which encourages the capitalist to invest again to earn higher profit, and the process goes on without any limit. Here lies the imbalance in the Western production system generated by limitless greed (Marx, 1978: 145-53).

The religious preachers, philosophers, and ethical intellectuals in the West could realize the danger of this psychosis of the capitalists. They strongly protested against this, but failed to devise any effective mechanism to restrain them. The unrestrained pursuit for earning more and more wealth easily overpowered all ethical preaching in the West. So material progress based on limitless greed went on unabated and intensified the inherent imbalance in the capitalistic production mechanism.

The Indian Traditional Path

The Indian traditional world outlook, as depicted in the ancient *śāstras* mentioned above, conceived of a balance in the process of material progress. It went into the basics of imbalance in the material living mode of human beings. The basic causes are defined in terms of the *ṛpus* or basic vices. The six major *ṛpus* are: *Kāma* (desire), *Krôdha* (anger), *Lôbha* (greed), *Moda* (pride), *Môha* (obsession), *Mātsarya* (jealousy). Excess of any of these elements brings about imbalance and disaster in human life.

All these *ṛpus* are essential for material existence of human beings but they must be kept under restrain. Otherwise they will generate imbalance in our life. We have already mentioned that the *ṛpu* of *Lôbha* (greed) is at the very root of imbalance in the West. Indian ethical approach is different from that of the West in the fact that it endeavoured to identify the basic causes of unethical human living in terms of the basic vices or *ṛpus*, and suggested means to keep the *ṛpus* under control. In all aspects of human life as taken into consideration by the ancient Indian *śāstras*, methods to control the *ṛpus* have been suggested directly or indirectly.

In Dharmaśāstras and Arthaśāstra of Kauṭilya, human living has been defined in terms of four *Puruṣārthas*, viz., *dharma*, *artha*, *kāma*, and *mōkṣa*. To control the influence of the powerful *ṛpus*, *kāma* (desire for material enjoyment) and *artha* (material and financial means to gratify the desires) are to be restrained by *dharma*. The final control of the *ṛpus* lies in the concept of *mōkṣa*, the spiritual achievements as the ultimate goal of human living, which is beyond material living.

The ancient Indian texts depict human development in terms of spiritual and ethical progress of men of all sorts, and in all walks of life. However, the texts never ignored material welfare of common people. All the Dharmaśāstras and the Arthaśāstra of Kauṭilya prescribed various provisions and welfare measures for amelioration of material living conditions of the masses that must be undertaken by the state.

These provisions are inseparable from human development efforts, but they themselves are not human development, which, according to ancient Indian literature, is the process of ethical and spiritual development of human beings (Radhakrishnan, 1966).

According to Indian philosophy, the creator *Brahman* is omnipresent but *Nirguṇa* (having no material characteristics). But human beings are *Saguṇa* (having specific characteristics) which are of three categories: (i) *Tamasa* (possessing '*Tama*' features); (ii) *Rajasa* (possessing '*Raja*' features) and (iii) *Sātvika* (possessing '*Satva*' features) (Panchamukhi, 2000: 33).

These three classes of people in the pure form may be distinguished on the basis of certain baser and nobler human attributes. Baser attributes include: greed, envy, hatred, anger, selfishness, lust, idleness, cruelty, pride etc. Nobler qualities, on the other hand, include: abstinence, self-sacrifice, love, philanthropy, mercy, self-confidence, diligence, composure etc. The baser features are of highest degree and nobler ones of lowest degree in a *Tamasa* man. For the *Rajasa* person, both types of features are of moderate degree and for the *Sātvika*, nobler qualities are of highest degree and baser ones completely absent (*ibid.* Ch. IV: 33-34).

Human development process, according to ancient Indian viewpoint, is a mechanism (self-imposed or imposed by society) that gradually reduces the intensities of *Tama* and *Raja* features and increases that of the *Satva* features in each person. It may not, however, be possible to eliminate the first two attributes completely and inculcate the third in full. But if it is possible to reduce the prevalence of the first two substantially from most of the people and enhance the influence of the third quality substantially among them, we would not be far from an ideal human society.

Thus, it becomes clear that human development in ancient Indian style is the most important task and without this, even improvement of material living conditions of the masses is not at all possible. Human development in terms of ethical and spiritual development of men – a journey from the *Tamasa* stage towards the *Sātvika* stage – is purely a qualitative matter and no quantitative indexing is possible here. In fact, indexing is not at all necessary for real human development endeavours.

Although the concept of India as a unified political entity existed since the Vedic times, successful effort in this regard was made for the first time during the reign of Chandra Gupta Maurya. Kauṭilya and his Arthaśāstra played a crucial role in this regard. Till the end of the reign of Aśoka the Great, there were mention-worthy endeavours to implement many economic, political and social policies on the basis of ancient Indian world outlook, particularly the ones prescribed in the Arthaśāstra. Later on, during the Gupta era, there was considerable geographical unification of India as a political entity, and at the peak of their glory, there was a resurgence of the efforts to study, rewrite and give real shape to ancient Indian world outlook. All these efforts, however, subsided with the decay of the Gupta era. Later on, there was a mild sign of revival during the rule of Harsa Vardhana, but it was only short lived. Since the first millennium the scenario changed completely. So far, the foreigners who had come to India did not have any strong ideologies. So, they could easily get assimilated with the mainstream of Indian culture, giving rise to a new enriched culture. But, the foreigners henceforth endeavoured to replace Indian tradition and culture by some alien culture. Though the age-old Indian traditional culture could withstand this continuous onslaught, much distortion resulted as a consequence of this continuous struggle. Along with foreign rule came the feudal system of the Middle East, which was contrary to ancient Indian tradition. Emergence of multiple mixed castes, degeneration of the Brahmin class, rapid spread of superstitions (many of them imported and others fabricated by the degenerated Brahmin class, or borrowed from the aboriginal cultures) etc. were also responsible for the degeneration of the Indian society.

During the British regime, administrative and economic reforms gave further blow to the Indian traditional culture. Permanent Settlement Policy of 1793 strengthened the roots of feudalism on Indian soil. The colonial rule by the British rulers resulted in abject poverty, famines and moral decay of the Indian society (Naoroji, 1901).

Since achievement of independence in 1947, the national government has been experimenting with various foreign ideas (both capitalistic and socialistic) for all round prosperity of India. But most of these foreign models have not been able to solve the basic problems facing the country, namely poverty, unemployment, degeneration of human values, social chaos, increasing incidence of crime, corruption in all spheres etc.

Now, the question arises whether a new path based on the traditional Indian world outlook could be relevant for solving our basic problems. In this study, we will try to investigate this matter. This is, however, a vast field of study calling for wide research at various levels and on various aspects. For our limited scope, we confine our study to two major ancient Indian texts, viz., Manusmṛti (the most prominent Dharmaśāstra) and Arthaśāstra of Kauṭilya.

We have already mentioned the place of Dharmaśāstras and Arthaśāstras in ancient Indian literature. A little more information about these texts is necessary since our study is based solely on these two texts.

Manusmṛti

Among the Dharmaśāstras, the text known as Manusmṛti occupies a very important place because of its wide coverage and detailed guidelines for various aspects of human living.

To quote:

> "Many myths have since very early times clustered round the name of Manu. He is regarded as perfect in study of the Veda, in the knowledge of its meaning, and the performance of its precepts. His origin is said to be divine and he is sometimes declared to be even a manifestation or incarnation of the Supreme Soul. ..."
>
> "Different Vedic works belonging to different Schools declare, 'All that Manu said is medicine, i.e., salutary.' He is said to be the fountain head of all the *Smṛtis* or traditional lore and Bṛhaspati, while proclaiming the superiority of Manu on the score of his strict adherence to the Veda, clearly declared that a text opposed to Manu is not commendable ..."
>
> "The *Paṇḍits* adhere to the above view up to the present time. This supreme position of the author justly commanded the unflinching adherence of the Hindus and made the work

exceptionally popular. The completeness of the work, its intelligibility and its orderly arrangement also contributed to the same result" (Sen, 1976: xii-xiii).

On the basis of evidence from ancient Indian texts the author of the present Manusmṛti flourished at least before 3000 B.C. (*ibid.*: xvi). The original Manusmṛti was written and revised several times later on to take account of the current problems of different ages. The original Manava Dharmaśāstra is likely to be different from the work which now goes by the name of Manu. It is clear from the fact that some of the *ślokas* attributed to Manu by Vasiṣṭha and others, are not to be found in the present text (*ibid.*: ix).

According to some authors, "The Manusmṛti had probably attained its present form by the 2nd century A.D. … We find that though the *Smṛtis* had begun at an early date and were supposed to have been based upon Vedic injunctions and customs, yet new *smṛti* authorities sprang up giving new injunctions which can hardly be traced to Vedic authorities. Many of the older authorities were again revised to harmonize the changes made and these revised editions passed off as the old ones as there was no critical apparatus of research for distinguishing the new from the old" (Dasgupta and Dey, 1962: xxvi).

There are also many *Vāṣyas* (commentaries) on Manusmṛti. The most popular available *Vāṣyas* are of Medhātithi, Kullūka Bhatta, Govindarāja, Sarvajña-Nārāyana, Rāghavānanda, Nandana, Rāmachandra and Gaṅgādhara. They reflect the transition in the methods for interpreting the text in accordance with the changes in values with changes in time.

Kautilya's Arthaśāstra

Before 1905, historians and scholars interested in ancient India did not have access to any reliable manuscript of Kauṭilya's Arthaśāstra. But references to this book were found in other available ancient Sanskrit literature, e.g., '*Nītisara*' of Kamandaka, '*Daśa Kumāra Charita*' of Dandin etc. (Shamaśāstry, 1967: vii-xiii). The existence of a manuscript of Kauṭilya's Arthasastra came to light in 1902 by Shamaśāstry, the then librarian of Oriental Manuscripts Library of Mysore, when it was handed over to the Library by a *Paṇḍit* of Tanjore district. Shamaśāstry produced a tentative English translation of the text in *Indian Antiquary* in 1905 and in the following years. The full text was edited and published by Shamaśāstry in 1909 (*ibid*.: v).

Comparing this text with citations and references in other ancient works, scholars and experts on ancient Indian literature agreed that Shamaśāstry's edition was really the copy of the work composed by Kauṭilya (Majumdar, 1960: 140). 'Though the existing text is, perhaps, not absolutely word for word that which was written by Kauṭilya' (*ibid.*:v).

It is apprehended that many sections of the original work have been lost and there might be some interpolations by authors belonging to later generations (*ibid.*:ix; also Sastrī, 1967: 200). Nevertheless, the available text is a rich and reliable source of research on Kauṭilya's economic and other ideas.

In the next chapter we will take up the guidelines for agriculture and land use as prescribed in the two texts, and their modern relevance.

References

Bible, Good News Edition, The Bible Society of India, Bangalore.

Chunder, P.C. (1995): *Kauṭilya Arthaśāstra*, The M.P. Birla Foundation, Calcutta.

Dasgupta, S.N. and Dey, S.K. (eds.) (1962): *A History of Sanskrit Literature*, Vol. I, University of Calcutta.

Graaff, J. de V. (1957): *Theoretical Welfare Economics*, Cambridge University Press, London.

Kangle, R.P. (1986): *Kauṭīlyan Arthaśāstra*, Part-II (English translation), Motilal Banarasidass, Delhi.

Majumdar, R.C. (1960): *Ancient India*, Motilal Banarasidass, Delhi.

Marx, K. (1978): *Capital, Volume I*, Progress Publishers, Moscow.

Naoroji, D. (1901): *Poverty and Un-British Rule in India*, Swan, Sonnenschein and Co. Ltd., London.

Panchamukhi, V.R. (2000): *Indian Classical Thoughts on Economic Development and Management*, Bookwell Publishers, New Delhi.

Radhakrishnan, S. (1966): *Indian Philosophy* (Vols.1, 2), George Allen and Unwin Ltd., New York Humanities Press, Inc., New York.

Sastri, K.A. Nilakanta (ed.) (1967): *Age of the Nandas and Mauryas*, Motilal Banarasidass, Delhi.

Sen, S.N. (1976): *Manusmṛti*, Chapter VII (English translation), Vidyodaya Series No.16, Chattopadhyaya Brothers, Calcutta.

Sen, A. (1999): *On Ethics and Economics*, Oxford University Press, New Delhi, Third Impression.

Shamaśāstry, R. (1967): *Kauṭilya's Arthaśāstra*, Mysore Printing and Publishing House, Mysore.

Smith, A. (1977): *An Inquiry Into the Nature and Causes of the Wealth of Nations*, Penguin Series.

Swāmī Śantī Dharamānanda Saraswatī (2000): *Sarvadarśan Sara* (in Hindi), Bharatīya Vidya Bhavan, Mumbai.

Manusmṛti

Sacred Books of the East, Vol. XXV, edited by F. Max Müller, Oxford Clarendon Press, 1886 (all quotations from Manusmṛti except those of Chapter 7 in this study are from this text; in quotations **8/1** means **Chapter 8**, ***śloka* 8)**

Manusmṛti, Chapter VII, (tr. Satyendra Nath Sen), Vidyodaya Series No.16, Chattopadhyaya Brothers, Calcutta, 1976 (all quotations of Chapter 7 from Manusmṛti in this study are from this book, in quotations **7/26** means **Chapter 7**, ***śloka* 26**)

Arthaśāstra

Kangle, R. P. (1986): *Kauṭīlyan Arthaśāstra*, Part-II (English translation), Motilal Banarasidass, Delhi.

(All quotations from Arthaśāstra in our study are from this text. In quotations **I/5/1** means **Book I, Chapter 5, *Śloka* 1** etc.)

3

Agriculture and Land Use

Eco-friendly and Sustainable Agricultural Pursuits

Agriculture is the main source of livelihood and national income in developing countries like India. So, economic development of these countries is not possible without sustainable development of the agricultural sector. Agriculture is dependent on availability of cultivable land, but land is also necessary for other purposes, e.g., habitation, forests, pasture grounds etc. Total available land in a country being limited, proper utilization of land, proper distribution of land among different uses, preservation of ecology of land etc. are essential for sustainable development of agriculture and all other sectors of the economy of a country (Dhingra, 2000: 309-18).

In ancient India, proper care was taken as regards the above matters. It may be argued that in ancient days agriculture was the main pre-occupation of the economy of a country and so it acquired utmost importance. But, in the modern era, industry is the driving force of an economy as it is free from the natural limitations of agriculture. Still, the importance of agriculture cannot be ignored altogether even in a modern economy. It is the sector that provides food and raw materials for many industries like textiles. In a country like India, agriculture has special importance as the majority of the population depend for their livelihoods on agriculture. It is true that we will have to depend ultimately on industry for rapid economic development of the country, but without a strong agricultural base, industrial development in a country like India may come up against serious bottlenecks. So along with industry, due importance should be attached to agriculture and allied activities also.

Now, let us see how these matters are handled in the two major ancient texts under consideration, viz., Manusmṛti and Arthaśāstra of Kauṭilya.

Manusmṛti

There are no specific guidelines regarding agriculture in Manusmṛti, which may be of use in modern India. It only mentions various rites to be performed for successful agricultural operations (as in the ***ślokas*** **4/26**; **4/27** and **4/28**). Manu considers that the profession of agriculture should not be undertaken by the two upper castes, viz., the Brāhmaṇa, and the *Kṣatriya* (as in the ***ślokas*** **10/83** and **10/84**).

It may be possible that he forbade agriculture for the *Brāhmaṇa* as agriculture means violence to the mother earth, which cannot be undertaken by a *Brāhmaṇa*. Besides these two aspects mentioned above, we do not get any specific guidelines about agriculture or land use from Manusmṛti. So, we will concentrate on the guidelines provided in the Arthaśāstra of Kauṭilya.

Arthaśāstra

In Kauṭilya's Arthasâstra, we get detailed guidelines regarding agriculture and proper land use. Kauṭilya asserts that prosperity of the country depends on agricultural development. He emphasizes the roles of agriculture and animal husbandry and elaborates on the merits of activities associated with these two sectors. Food and many essential articles for human living come from these sectors. He also opines that the strength of a country *vis-à-vis* its enemy country depends on the soundness of these activities.

To quote:

I/4/1: Agriculture, cattle-rearing and trade – these constitute economics, (which are) beneficial, as they yield grains, cattle, money, forest produce and labour.

I/4/2: Through them, the (king) brings under his sway his own party as well as the party of the enemies, by the (use of the) treasury and the army.

According to Kauṭilya agriculture should be a profession of the *Vaiśyas*.

To quote:

I/3/7: Those of the *Vaiśya* are: studying, performing sacrifices for self, making gifts, agriculture, cattle-rearing and trade.

Under certain circumstances he also prescribes agricultural activities by *Śūdras*, especially in newly established villages.

To quote:

II/1/2: He should cause villages to be settled consisting mostly of *Śūdra* agriculturists, with a minimum of one hundred families and a maximum of five hundred families, with boundaries extending over one *krośa* or two *krośas*, (and) affording mutual protection.

The measures to be undertaken by the king for agricultural development and proper land use are prescribed in the following manner. These consist of rules for settlement in the countryside (old or new), selection of appropriate persons who are to be entrusted with the task of land development, how land is to be distributed for various uses like agriculture, pastures, factories, forests, water reservoirs and irrigation networks, habitations etc. Kauṭilya also prescribes measures for encouraging private persons efficient in activities pertaining to agriculture and proper land use, and punitive measures for those who violate rules in this regard or create obstruction to these activities.

It is an important question how to develop land in the hitherto uncultivated areas. It is quite natural that without government initiative and encouragement, people on their own would not be interested in settling in these areas. So, Kauṭilya prescribes state-sponsored schemes for developing land for cultivation in these areas.

One way of development of hitherto uncultivated land was to provide tax concessions to those who were willing to cultivate the uncultivated land.

To quote:

II/1/8: He should allot to tax-payers arable fields for life.

II/1/9: Unarable fields should not be taken away from those who are making them arable.

If any person left the land given to him uncultivated, the state should promptly seize it and hand it over to some diligent cultivator. Also these persons were to pay compensations for keeping land idle. This was a strong measure to discourage misuse of land resources of the country. The energetic cultivators should also be encouraged by the state through grants and loans. To quote:

II/1/10: He should take away (fields) from those who do not till them and give them to others.

II/1/11: Or, village servants and traders should till them.

II/1/12: Or, those who do not till should make good the loss (to the treasury).

II/1/13: And he should favour them with grains, cattle and money.

II/1/14: These they should pay back afterwards at their convenience.

Kauṭilya also associates various allied activities with agricultural pursuits and prescribes the role of the state in encouraging these activities. Along with agricultural activities, the state should sponsor and encourage activities associated with development of general forests, forests suitable for living of elephants and other wild animals, pasture lands, and also marketing, and transportation and communications facilities. In fact all these are interrelated and for proper development a holistic approach is necessary. Kauṭilya was wise enough to realize that a single activity cannot properly flourish in isolation.

To quote:

II/1/19: He should set going work in mines, factories, produce-forests, elephant-forests, cattle-herds and trade routes and (establish) water routes, land routes and ports.

II/2/1: On land unsuitable for agriculture, he should allot pastures for cattle.

Kauṭilya prescribes measures for irrigation facilities which are essential for development of agriculture. For this purpose, he suggests construction of water reservoirs, wells, tanks, fountains etc. Trees should be planted for soil and water conservation, especially in dry areas. In this regard, the state should also seek people's participation. People undertaking these activities should be encouraged by the state in various ways.

To quote:

II/1/20: He should cause irrigation works to be built with natural water sources or with water to be brought in from elsewhere.

II/1/21: Or, to others who are building (these), he should render aid with land, road, trees and implements, and (also render aid) to (the building of) holy places and parks.

II/1/23: And he should be a sharer in the expenses and yet should receive no portion (of the benefits derived).

II/34/8: In waterless regions, he should establish wells, water works and springs, also flower and fruit enclosures.

III/9/33: When tanks and embankments are newly constructed, an exemption (from taxes) for five years (should be granted), when those that are ruined and abandoned are renovated, an exemption for four years, when those that are overgrown with weeds are cleared, for three years, when dry land is newly brought under cultivation, for two years.

III/9/34: He is free to mortgage or sell.

III/10/46: The king should do what is agreeable and beneficial to these, when they build dykes that are of benefit to the country or bridges on roads or carry out works beautifying the villages or defences (of the villages).

How various crops are to be cultivated are described in detail in **II/24**. Here Kauṭilya describes how different crops are to be planted according to the specificity of soil and weather conditions. Varieties of the same crops (depending on specific conditions) are also mentioned. On the whole agriculture, according to Kauṭilya, is to be eco-friendly and sustainable; and there should be a proper balance among different kinds of uses of scarce land.

All varieties of seeds are to be collected in proper time and preserved properly.

To quote:

II/24/1: The Director of Agriculture, himself conversant with the practice of agriculture, water-dividing and the science of rearing plants, or assisted by experts in these, should collect, in the proper seasons, seeds of all kinds of grains, flowers, fruits, vegetables, bulbous roots, roots, creeper fruits, flax, and cotton.

Crops are to be sown according to appropriateness of soils, climatic conditions etc.

To quote:

II/24/2: He should cause them to be sown in land, suitable for each, which has been ploughed many times, through serfs, labourers and persons paying off their fines by personal labour.

II/24/11: In conformity with that, he should cause crops to be sown, requiring plenty of water or little water.

II/24/15: Or, the sowing of seeds (should be) in conformity with the season.

II/24/19: According to the amount of water (available) for the work, he should decide on wet crops, winter crops or summer crops.

II/24/22: (A region) where the foam strikes (the banks) is (suited) for creeper fruits, (regions on) the outskirts of overflows, for long pepper, grapes and sugarcanes, (those on) the borders of wells, for vegetables and roots, (those on) the borders of moist beds of lakes, for green grasses, ridges for plants reaped by cutting, (such as) perfume plants, medicinal herbs, *uśīra*-grass, *hrībera*, *piṇḍāluka* and others.

II/24/23: And on lands suitable for each, he should raise plants that grow on dry lands and those that grow in wetlands.

The proper condition for growth of crops is described in the following ***ślokas***.

II/24/10: Where it rains distributing wind and sunshine properly and creating three (periods for the drying of) cowdung cakes, there the growth of crops is certain.

Kauṭilya describes the order of crops to be grown so as to maintain a balance in fertility of soil and ecology.

To quote:

II/24/12: *śāli*-rice, *vrīhi*-rice, *kodrava*, sesamum, *priyaṅgu*, *udāraka* and *varaka* are the first sowings.

II/24/13: *mudga*, *māṣa* and *śaimbya* are the middle sowings.

II/24/14: Safflower, lentils, *kulattha*, barley, wheat, *kalāya*, linseed and mustard are the last sowings.

Kauṭilya also describes how seeds are to be prepared before sowing, and how crop saplings are to be properly maintained.

To quote:

II/24/24: Soaking in dew (by night) and drying in the heat (by day) for seven days and nights (is the treatment) in the case of seeds of grains, for three days and nights or five in the case of seeds of pulses, smearing at the cut with honey, ghee and pig's fat, mixed with cowdung in the case of stalks that serve as seeds, (smearing) with honey and ghee in the case of bulbous roots, smearing with cowdung in the case of stone-like seeds, (and) in the case of trees, burning in the pit and fulfillment of the longing with cow bones and cowdung at the proper time.

II/24/25: And when they have sprouted, he should feed them with fresh acrid fish along with the milk of the *snuhi*-plant.

Kauṭilya prescribes some natural devices to drive out serpents from the crop field.

To quote:

II/24/26: He should collect (and burn) the seeds of cotton and the slough of a serpent. Serpents do not remain where there is this smoke.

Relevance for Modern India

Although it cannot be denied that future rapid development of the Indian economy depends mainly on the growth of the industrial sector and agricultural sector is to play only a supporting role, the overwhelming importance of the agricultural sector in the Indian economy can by no means be ignored. It is still the source of livelihood of more than sixty percent of the population and a large part of the national income of the country comes from this sector. Moreover, agriculture is the basic source of food and many industrial raw materials like cotton, jute etc. The Government of India and the Planning Commission had to learn this the hard way. Because of neglect of agricultural sector during the Second Five-Year Plan (1956-61), food shortages took a serious turn during the sixties and the situation had to be met by massive food grains imports from the USA under the PL-480 aid programme. Since the mid-sixties, experiments were made with the new agricultural technology under Intensive District Programme. This ultimately led to spectacular increase in wheat production, especially in Punjab, Haryana and western Uttar Pradesh. This incident was termed by many as ‘Green Revolution’. The major ingredients of the new agricultural technology are: HYV (High Yielding Varieties) seeds, intensive irrigation, application of high doses of chemical fertilizers and pesticides, and use of modern implements like tractors, harvesters etc. Later on, application of the new technology spread to other food crops like paddy, jowar etc., and to various commercial crops. The geographical coverage of the new technology also increased over time. Rapid growth of production of food grains enabled India to do away with food imports (*ibid.:* 349-69).

In spite of the apparent success of the new agricultural technology as described above, the following long-term adverse consequences of this technology can by no means be overlooked.

(a) Long-term adverse effects on soil and water of too much use of chemical fertilizers and pesticides.
(b) Pollution of underground water by chemical fertilizers and pesticides.
(c) Too much use of underground water for irrigation leading to serious ecological hazards and arsenic pollution.
(d) Loss of natural seed varieties suitable for various climatic conditions and with natural capability to resist the attacks of pests and diseases. India has already lost most of its natural seed varieties by indiscriminately copying the Western practice of using hybrid seeds, which lack the natural capability to resist the vagaries of climate and attack of germs and pests (*ibid.*: 354, 358-59).

Now, the question arises whether we are likely to get any fruitful guidelines from *Arthaśāstra* of Kauṭilya regarding solution of these problems. The following lessons from this text may be relevant for India today.

1. ***Ślokas*** **II/1/8-14** above suggest that direct relation between actual cultivators and the state, and state encouragement and help to small owner-cultivators, are likely to be beneficial for both the cultivators and agriculture. This emphasizes the importance of land reforms, which is an urgent necessity for India at present.
2. We may get an idea of proper use of uncultivable land from the ***śloka*** **II/2/1** above.

3. The high yielding varieties of seeds (as used under modern agricultural technology in India at present) are vulnerable to various plant diseases, and are not suitable for all sorts of climatic and soil conditions. So, following Kauṭilya's guidelines (***śloka*** **II/24/1** above) we may carry out research on how varieties of crop-seeds suitable for varieties of situations may be collected and preserved. If proper research is undertaken, high level of production may be possible by using natural seeds alone and there would be no necessity of using problematic so called HYV seeds.
4. Large irrigation projects have failed to serve the intended purpose in India during the plan period. On the contrary, they have generated flood situations and other ecological problems. The deep tube-well irrigation system, which was praised so much in the beginning, has now been considered as the source of various ecological damages associated with underground water erosion, arsenic poisoning etc.

   In the ***ślokas*** **II/1/20-23**, **II/34/8**, **III/9/33-34** and **III/10/46** above, we find that Kauṭilya suggests regional reservoirs with mass participation. This is likely to create self-help among people, generate employment and also create eco-friendly irrigation networks. If local reservoirs are constructed by mass participation in many different locations along the course of rivers, and also in inland areas with heavy rainfall, river water could be collected in rainy season (preventing flood), and water stagnation (in rainy season) in inland areas with heavy rainfall could easily be avoided. Moreover, in dry seasons, agriculture would not suffer from lack of water.
5. ***Ślokas*** **II/24/24-26** indicate a field of research to find out means to make crops as disease free as possible without using eco-damaging pesticides.

In recent years, there has fortunately been increasing awareness to device means to make agricultural practices eco-friendly and sustainable. The Central Government and various state governments have recently been emphasizing on retrieval of our traditional knowledge so as to make agriculture in India eco-friendly and sustainable. Brief outlines of these policy changes are given below:

Organic Farming

Organic farming system is not new in India and is being followed from ancient time. It is a method of farming system which primarily aimed at cultivating land and raising crops in such a way as to keep the soil alive and in good health by use of organic wastes (crop, animal and farm waste, aquatic waste) and other biological material along with beneficial microbes (bio-fertilizers) to release nutrients to crops for increased sustainable production in an eco-friendly, pollution-free environment.

Components

Basically, organic farming components can be grouped into five categories: (a) green manures; (b) crop rotation; (c) organic manures (farm yard manure, compost, vermicompost); (d) bio-pesticides; and (e) bio-fertilizers.

Benefits

(a) Helps in maintaining environment health by reducing the level of pollution.
(b) Reduces human and animal hazards by reducing the level of residue in the product.
(c) Increases the agricultural products and makes them sustainable.

(d) Ensures the optimum utilisation of natural resources for short-term benefit and helps in conserving them for future generation.

(e) Saves energy for both animal and machine and reduces the risk of crop failure.

(f) Improves the physical and chemical properties of soil.

(g) Besides the point given above, it has been demonstrated extensively that plant products from organic farming are substantially better in quality as they are bigger in size, look, flavour and aroma. Animal products are also better in quality when they are fed with feed and fodder produced organically. The underground water of the area where such farming system is in practice has been found to be free of toxic chemicals.

Bio-fertilizers

Bio-fertilizers are ready-to-use live formulates of such beneficial microorganism, which, on application to seed, root or soil, mobilize the availability of nutrients by their biological activity in particular and help build up the micro flora and in turn, the soil health in general.

Nitrogenous bio-fertilizers harvest atmosphere nitrogen and convert it into ammonical form, which in due course is made available to the plants or is released in the soil. Phosphate solutions make soluble fixed forms of phosphorus already present in the soil and make it available for use of plants. Compositing bio-fertilizers are used for hastening the process of compositing and for enriching its nutrient value.

With the introduction of green revolution technologies modern agriculture is getting more and more dependent upon the steady supply of synthetic inputs (mainly fertilizers), which are products of fossil fuel (coal+ petroleum). Excessive dependence of modern agriculture on the supply of these synthetic inputs and the adverse effects being noticed due to their excessive and imbalanced use has compelled the scientific fraternity to look for alternatives.

Some of the points of concern are:

(i) Availability and cost:

  (a) Demand is much higher than the availability. It is estimated that by 2020, to achieve the targeted production of 321 million tonnes of food grain, the requirement of nutrient will be 28.8 million tonnes, while their availability will be only 21.6 million tonnes. Thus there will be a deficit of about 7.2 million tonnes.

  (b) Increasing costs are becoming unaffordable for small and marginal farmers.

(ii) Effect of chemical fertilizers in soil and environment:

  (a) Excessive and imbalanced use of chemical fertilizers has adversely affected the soil causing decrease in organic carbon, reduction in microbial flora of soil, increasing acidity and alkalinity, and hardening of soil.

  (b) Excessive use of N-fertilizer are contaminating water bodies thus affecting fish fauna and causing health hazards for human beings and animals.

  (c) Production of chemical fertilizers adds to pollution.

To overcome the deficit in nutrient supply and to overcome the adverse effects of chemical cultivation it is suggested that efforts should be made to exploit all the available resources of nutrients under the scheme of integrated nutrient management. Under this approach the best available option lies in the complimentary use of bio-fertilizers and organic manures in suitable combination of chemical fertilizers.

This integrated approach of nutrient management not only ensures higher productivity but also ensures the good health of our soil and environment. Bio-fertilizers are essential components of this approach and are being promoted to harvest the naturally available biological system of nutrient mobilization.

Benefits

Use of bio-fertilizers will:

(a) Increase crop yield by 20-30 per cent

(b) Replace chemical Nitrogen and Phosphorus by 25 per cent

(c) Stimulate plant growth

(d) Activate soil biologically

(e) Restore natural fertility

(f) Provide protection against drought and some soil-borne diseases.

Types of Bio-fertilizers

- **For Nitrogen:** Rhizobium for legume crops; Azotobacter/ Azospirillum for non-legume crops; Acetobacter for sugarcane only; BGA and Azolla for low land paddy;
- **For Phosphorous:** Phosphatika for all crops to be applied with Rhizobium, Azotobacter, Azospirillum and Acetobacter.
- **For enriched compost:** Cellulolytic fungal culture; Phosphotika and Azotobacter culture.

Recommendations

(a) For pulses such as *moong*, *urad*, *arhar* etc. and legume oil seeds such as groundnut and soyabean, use Rhizobium + Phosphotika 200 gm each per 10 kg of seed as seed treatment.

(b) For non-legume crops such as wheat, sorghum, maize, cotton, mustard etc., use Azotobacter + Phosphotika 200 gm each per 10 kg of seed as seed treatment.

(c) For Jute – Azospirillum + Phosphotika 200 gm each as seed treatment.

(d) For vegetables like tomato, brinjal, chilli, cabbage, cauliflower etc. use Azotobacter/Azospirillum + Phosphotika, 1 kg each.

(e) For low land transplanted paddy use Azospirillum + Phosphotika 2 kg each/acre.

(f) For potato, ginger colocassia, turmeric, sugarcane and zoom paddy use Azospirillum/Azotobacter + Phosphotika 4 kg each/acre mixed with compost and applied as soil treatment.

(g) For sugarcane use Acetobacter + Phosphotika 4 kg each/acre.

(h) For plantation crops use Azotobacter – Phosphotika 4 kg each/acre with compost and applied in soil in two splits per year.

Method of Application

Seed treatment: Suspend 200 gm N-bio-fertilizer and 200 gms Phosphotika in 300-400 ml of water and mix thoroughly. Mix this paste with 10 kg seeds and dry in shade. Sow immediately.

Seedling root dip: For vegetables 1 kg each of two bio-fertilizers should be mixed in sufficient quantity of water. Dip the roots of seedlings in this suspension for 30-40 min before transplanting. For paddy make a bed in the field and fill it with water. Mix bio-fertilizers in water and dip the roots of seedlings for 8-10 hrs.

Soil treatment: Mix 4 kg each of bio-fertilizers in 200 kg of compost and leave it overnight. Apply this mixture in the soil at the time of sowing or planting.

In plantation crops apply this mixture near root zone and cover with soil.

Precautions

Store bio-fertilizer packets in a cool and dry place away from direct sunlight and heat. Use the right combination of bio-fertilizers. Rhizobium is crop specific, so use in the specified crop. Do not mix with chemicals. While purchasing ensure that each packet is provided with necessary information like name of the product, name of the crop for which intended, name and address of the manufacturer, date of manufacture, date of expiry, batch number and instructions for use. Use the packet before expiry, only on the specified crop, and by the recommended method.

From the above analysis we see that the so-called "Bio-Farming" is basically the methods practiced in ancient India, and we have already seen that Arthaśāstra is a rich source of knowledge for this type of eco-friendly agriculture (for details see the website: http://manipur.nic.in/rbdc/FarmerInfo.htm).

Food Security Policy of Government of India

The Food Security Policy (2000) of the Government of India also emphasized retrieval of ancient knowledge of eco-friendly agriculture. [see the website http://www.baif.com/ additional_ tree8.htm]. The relevant aspects are described below in brief:

Extension of Traditional Wisdom

For ensuring sustainable agriculture, it is advisable to explore the traditional wisdom and promote local practices. The study of local traditions will help in understanding the soil fertility and water management systems developed over years. As these practices have helped in the past to produce enough food grains before the introduction of chemical fertilizers, sustainable agriculture can be promoted on these traditions. Thus sustainable farming is the extension of traditional practices with necessary modifications. But there has been an increase in agricultural byproducts and domestic garbage, which can be used for composting. With the promotion of agro-forestry, live hedges and wind breaks, it is possible to produce biomass useful for green manure. Cultivation of green manure crop of short duration between two crops is another option to enhance soil fertility. Adaptation of dairy farming with high yielding cattle and buffaloes, stalk feeding and installation of biogas plants can generate significant quantity of farmyard manure, while generating additional income and energy. Use of earthworms can further improve the quality of the manure.

The soil productivity can be further enhanced through soil and water conservation, improved drainage, contour bunding and establishment of live hedges. In arid and semiarid regions where the use of chemical fertilizers is risky, application of organic manure and bio-fertilizers, adoption of tree-based farming, coupled with improved drought tolerant crop varieties and integrated pest management can be promoted to boost the yields. These include the use of efficient irrigation systems, bio-fertilizers, bio-pesticides, safe agrochemicals and improved seeds, which have direct bearing on crop yields and cost of production. Simple techniques for soil, water and plant analysis to maintain nutritional balance, and weed and pest management to reduce nutrient losses are some areas where technology transfer has been lagging behind. Farmers can be oriented to make judicious use of nutrients based on the soil fertility, organic matter content, soil moisture availability and the crop requirement, as the balance between organic manure, macro- and micro-nutrients is very critical to induce flowering and crop yields.

Bio-Technology Policy of MP Government

The bio-technology policy, 2003 of the Madhya Pradesh government is also mentionworthy in this regard (http://www.mpbiotech.gov.in/BDPolicy.html). The relevant segments are given below:

Traditional Knowledge and Wisdom and Awareness Generation

Madhya Pradesh is rich in its biotic resources. Rural and tribal communities have, over time, through proper selection, elimination and locally evolved techniques, developed a vast range of applications and practices which add value to agricultural and forest produce. Steps to help protect the rights of the community over this traditional knowledge base shall be initiated. Partnerships between rural and tribal communities and research institutions shall be established to improve and expand the applications environment for traditional knowledge and practices. A strategy to derive advantage for these communities under the various statutory provisions of enactments like the Environmental Protection Act, the Wildlife Protection Act, the Plant Varieties and Farmers Rights Protection Act, the Biological Diversity Act, the Indian Patents Act etc. shall be prepared. Modern tools of bio-technology can help enhance the potential of traditional knowledge and practices. This will help in improved production, value addition and promoting the sustainable use of natural resources.

Recent Agriculture Policy of Tamil Nadu Government

The recent agriculture policy of the Tamil Nadu government reflects its concern about the problems generated by modern agricultural technology and here also there has been an emphasis on seeking the solution in our traditional technologies. The brief outline of their policy is delineated below (for detail see the website: http://www.tn.gov.in/policynotes/agriculture_2.htm):

1. The change in land use pattern created serious concern among the agricultural planners to evolve suitable development strategies. The fallow lands increased from 22.93 lakh ha. during 1990-91 to 28.17 lakh ha. during 2003-04.

The gross cropped area declined to 53.16 lakh ha. during 2003-04 from the average normal coverage of 63 lakh ha. leaving about 9.8 lakh ha. fallow.

2. Though the reduction of cropped area during 2003-04 was evidently more due to the acute drought that prevailed during that year, still there was reduction under gross cropped area to the tune of around 4 lakh ha. between 1990-91 to 2001-02. The major problems facing agriculture of the state are: pre-dominance of dryland areas, overexploitation of irrigation sources, deterioration of soil health due to continuous intensive cropping, shrinking trend of gross cropped area and also continuous severe drought.
3. The strategies of the government to achieve the goals in the agricultural sector are: adoption of alternative cropping strategies derived for agro-climatic zone-based cropping pattern evolved by TNAU to raise remunerative crops and to ensure maximum utilization of available land and water aiming at increasing cropping intensity.
4. Taking up cultivation in vast tract of wastelands through Massive Comprehensive Waste Land Development Programme.
5. Adoption of dry land development technologies and crop production technologies for dry land crops to step up their productivity.
6. Massive adoption of integrated nutrient management and integrated pest management technology with emphasis on eco-friendly agriculture development.
7. Much focus on restoration of soil through organic farming approach and to promote vermi composting, compost making through plueorotus, green manuring etc. Efforts to provide site specific macro- and micro-nutrient recommendations on the basis of soil test villagewise fertility Index.
8. Promotion of microirrigation to maximize water use efficiency.

The policy makers of the central government and the state governments in India would be highly benefited if they look deeply into the prescriptions regarding agriculture in the Arthaśāstra of Kauṭilya. The present policy makers have become aware of the various dangers of the blind adoption of western technologies to step up agricultural production and productivity in India. It has been realized that such a growth process of agriculture is neither sustainable nor eco-friendly. In all these respects prescriptions in the Arthaśāstra of Kauṭilya will definitely be of considerable help and would provide guidelines for solving various other problems associated with Indian agriculture today. However, suitable modifications of Kauṭilya's policies may be necessary in accordance with the objective conditions of modern India.

To conclude, we strongly assert that in essence Kauṭilya's guidelines discussed above are fully relevant today although proper research works may be necessary to make them applicable in the present conditions.

References

Dhingra, I.C. (2000): *The Indian Economy*, Sultan Chand and Sons, New Delhi.

Websites:

(http://manipur.nic.in/rbdc/FarmerInfo.htm)

(http://www.mpbiotech.gov.in/BDPolicy.html)

(http://www.tn.gov.in/policynotes/agriculture_2.htm)

(http://www.baif.com/additional_tree8.htm)

4

Environment and Ecology

Holistic Approach to Environment and Ecology

In the modern era, awareness about environment and ecology arose only since the middle of the twentieth century. In fact, the current wave of environment awareness got a fillip only after the United Nations Conference on Human Environment held in 1972 at Stockholm (Sweden), and the matter gained further importance after the Earth Summit held in 1992 at Rio de Janeiro (Brazil). But long ago, in ancient Indian texts, we find this awareness pertaining to the preservation of environment and ecology of this planet Earth. Now, let us discuss in detail the prescriptions and viewpoints in this regard as delineated in two important ancient Indian texts, viz., Manusmṛti and Arthaśāstra of Kauṭilya.

Manusmṛti

The ecological principles of Manusmṛti are based on the basic ideal of the Upaniṣads, "*Vasudhaiva kūtumbakam*", i.e., all the beings of the entire universe belong to the same family. By means of defining cosmology, Manu here endeavours to spell out the basic sources of interrelationship among all beings in this universe as in the following *ślokas*:

Manu describes how all the material (and perishable) things (living beings as well as lifeless matters) of the world have originated from the same five elements or *Pancha-bhutas* (*Khiti* (Earth), *Ap* (Water), *Teza* (Fire), *Marut* (Air) and *Byom* (Sky).

To quote:

1/27: But with the minute perishable particles of the five (elements) which have been mentioned, this whole (world) is framed in due order.

1/38: Lightning, thunderbolts and clouds, imperfect (*rohita*) and perfect rainbows, falling meteors, supernatural noises, comets, and heavenly lights of many kinds.

1/39: (Horsed-faced) *Kinnaras*, monkeys, fishes, birds of many kinds, cattle, deer, men and carnivorous beasts with two rows of teeth.

1/40: Small and large worms and beetles, moths, lice, flies, bugs, all stinging and biting insects and the several kinds of immovable things.

1/46: All plants, propagated by seed or by slips, grow from shoots; annual plants (are those) which, bearing many flowers and fruits, perish after the ripening of their fruit.

1/47: (Those trees) which bear fruit without flowers are called *Vanaspati* (lords of the forest); but those which bear both flowers and fruits are called *Vṛkṣa*.

1/48: But the various plants with many stalks, growing from one or several roots, the different kinds of grasses, the climbing plants and the creepers, all spring from seed or from slips.

1/49: These (plants) which are surrounded by multiform darkness, the result of their acts (in former existences), possess internal consciousness and experience pleasure and pain.

Manu opines that all material things are transitory and get reduced to the basic elements. But only the creator is imperishable and permanent. All the material things are created, destroyed, and again created in a cyclical way by the immortal creator.

To quote:

1/57: Thus he, the imperishable one, by (alternately) waking and slumbering, incessantly revivifies and destroys this whole movable and immovable (creation).

In this way Manu goes in depth into the reason why we should try to conform to the harmony of the whole universe ordained by the creator. So, ecological awareness in Manu is not at all *ad hoc* but relates to some limited self-preserving requirements of the human race. The specific guidelines prescribed by Manu on the basis of the above realization are discussed below.

The guidelines for harmonious living with the orderly universe are described in the following *ślokas*. Here Manu also prescribes various rites to get rid of the sin committed to nature and its universal ecology since he looks upon all these matters from moral and religious standards.

3/68: A householder has five slaughter-houses (as it were, viz.), the hearth, the grinding-stone, the broom, the pestle and mortar, and the water-vessel, by using which he is bound (with the fetters of sin).

3/69: In order to successively expiate (the offences committed by means) of these, the five-great sages have prescribed for householders a scheme of the daily (performance of the five) sacrifices. In the upper storey let him offer a *Bali* to *Sarvātmabhūti*; but let him throw what remains (from these offerings) in a southerly direction for the manes.

3/88: Saying '(Adoration) to the *Maruts*', he shall scatter (some food) near the door, and (some) in water, saying, '(Adoration) to the water', he shall throw (some) on the pestle and the mortar, speaking thus, '(Adoration) to the trees'.

3/91: Let him make *Bali* offering in the upper storey (or, beside house) unto '*Sarvātmabhūti*', and then unto the (departed) fathers from what remains, towards the south.

3/92: Let him place on the ground (some food) for dogs, outcastes, *caṇḍālas* (*śvapak*), those afflicted with diseases that are punishments for former sins, crows and insects.

3/93: That *Brāhmaṇa* who thus daily honours all beings, goes, endowed with a resplendent body, by a straight road to the highest dwelling-place (i.e., *Brahman*).

Besides these religious way of conforming with the ethical requirements of harmonious living, Manu also prescribes rules directly connected with day-to-day activities of different classes of people. But here Manu does not like to use coercive power of law or the state. He simply endeavours to make people behave properly and in a harmonious way by moral suasion, and fear of being punished by the laws of the creator. These were likely to have a stronger and more sustainable effect than that achieved by legal restrictions – one may cheat the eyes of law but not that of the creator. The most prestigious caste is the Brahmin and for him it is an urgent necessity (as others are to learn from him), to live by means which perpetrates the least possible harm to others. This may be exempted only when he is in distress.

To quote:

4/2: A *Brāhmaṇa* must seek a means of subsistence which either causes no, or at least little pain (to others), and live (by that) except in times of distress.

5/43: A twice-born man of virtuous disposition, whether he dwells in (his own) house, with a teacher, or in the forest, must never, even in times of distress, cause an injury (to any creature) which is not sanctioned by the Veda.

5/45: He who injures innoxious beings from a wish to (give) himself pleasure, never finds happiness, neither living nor dead.

5/46: He who does not seek to cause the sufferings of bonds and death to living creatures (but) desires the good of all (beings) obtains endless bliss.

4/238: Giving no pain to any creature, let him slowly accumulate spiritual merit, for the sake (of acquiring) a companion to the next world, just as the white ant (gradually raises its) hill.

Manu tries to prevent people from voiding urine in places other than the urinals (or any appropriate place specified for that purpose) by publicizing the following viewpoint about the consequences of such misdeeds.

4/52: The intellect of (a man) who voids urine against a fire, the sun, the moon, in water, against a *Brāhmaṇa*, a cow, or the wind, perishes.

The following *śloka* is intended to prevent water pollution by uncivic behaviour of people.

4/56: Let him not throw urine or faeces into the water, nor saliva, nor (clothes) defiled by impure substances, nor any other (impurity), nor blood, nor poisonous things.

The following *śloka* is intended to make people follow the proper way of maintenance of cleanliness in the day-to-day household life.

4/151: Far from his dwelling let him remove urine (and ordure), far (let him remove) the waters used for washing his feet, and far the remnants of food and the water from his bath.

To prevent unnecessary killing of animals, Manu opines that meat-eating should be restricted to only specific purposes. He also suggests some alternatives how strong desire for meat could be fulfilled by simulation.

To quote:

5/34: After death the guilt of one who slays deer for gain is not as (great) as that of him who eats meat for no (sacred) purpose.

5/37: If he has a strong desire (for meat) he may make an animal of clarified butter or one of flour, (and eat that); but let him never seek to destroy an animal without a (lawful) reason.

In the following *śloka*, Manu specifies the specific case where meat eating and killing of animals may be permissible.

5/41: On offering the honey-mixture (to a guest), at a sacrifice and at the rites in honour of the manes, but on these occasions only, may an animal be slain; that (rule) *Manu* proclaimed.

Manu describes in the following *śloka* the consequences of killing, destroying or injuring various types of living beings. This was intended to preserve bio-diversity.

11/69: Killing a donkey, a horse, a camel, a deer, an elephant, a goat, a sheep, a fish, a snake, or a buffalo, must be known to degrade (the offender) to a mixed caste (*Saṃkarikaraṇa*).

11/71: Killing insects, small or large, or birds, eating anything kept close to spirituous liquors, stealing fruit, firewood, or flowers, (are offences) which make impure (*Malāvaha*).

In the following *ślokas*, Manu prescribes certain practical measures for maintenance of ecology of the villages, towns and other places of human habitation.

8/237: On all sides of a village a space, one hundred *dhanus* or three *samyâ*-throws (in breadth), shall be reserved (for pasture), and thrice (that space) round a town.

8/246: Let him mark the boundaries (by) trees, (e.g.) *Nyagrodhas*, *Aśvatthas*, *Kimśukas*, cotton-trees, *Śālas*, Palmyra palms, and trees with milky juice.

8/247: By clustering shrubs, bamboos of different kinds, *Śamīs*, creepers and raised mounds, reeds, thickets of *Kubjaka*; thus the boundary will not be forgotten.

8/248: Tanks, wells, cisterns, and fountains should be built where boundaries meet, as well as temples.

Manu realized that moral suasions and religious preaching may not be sufficient to prevent all people from doing eco-damaging mischief. So, sometimes it may be necessary to prevent them by legal and punitive measures by the state. In the following *ślokas*, Manu mentions legal and punitive measures against the violators of rules pertaining to the preservation of environment and ecology.

9/281: But he who shall take away the water of a tank, made in ancient times, or shall cut off the supply of water, must be made to pay the first (or lowest) amercement.

9/282: But he who, except in a case of extreme necessity, drops filth on the king's high-road, shall pay two *Kārṣāpaṇas* and immediately remove (that) filth.

9/283: But a person in urgent necessity, an aged man, a pregnant woman, or a child, shall be reprimanded and clean the (place); that is a settled rule.

From the above discussion, it becomes clear that Manu's approach towards environment and ecology was a holistic one, where he treated these problems as a part of the cosmic harmony.

Arthaśāstra

Kauṭilya is more matter of fact and thorough than Manu as regards protection and maintenance of environment and ecology. The task of protecting forests and other natural resources is entrusted with the king (through different state officials), appropriate plants should be grown to protect dry lands and pasture lands should be properly protected. The king should protect different types of forests, water reservoirs and mines.

To quote:

II/1/39: Thus the king should protect the produce-forests, elephant-forests, irrigation works and mines that were made in ancient times and should start new ones.

II/2/4: And he should establish on its border or in conformity with the (suitability of the) land, another animal park where all animals are (welcomed) as guests (and given full protection).

II/2/5: And, he should establish forests, one each for the products indicated as forest produce …

II/2/6: On the border (of the kingdom), he should establish a forest for elephants guarded by foresters.

II/2/7: The superintendent of the elephant-forest should, with the help of guards of the elephant-forest, protect the elephant-forest (whether) on the mountain, along a river, along lakes or in marshy tracts, with its boundaries, entrances and exits (fully) known.

II/2/8: They should kill anyone slaying an elephant.

Houses and other dwelling places, roads, cremation grounds etc. should be properly constructed preserving environment. Every house should have proper arrangements for controlling fire. Any violation of the rules pertaining to these matters would make one liable to punishment.

To quote:

II/4/1: Three royal highways running west to east and three running south to north, that should be the division of the residential area.

Every house should be constructed strictly on the basis of the rules (for preserving environment) prescribed by the authorities. There should be proper arrangements in each house for sewage and proper disposal of wastes. The violators would be fined according to the gravity of the offence.

III/8/6: (He should make) the dung-hill, the water-course or the well, not in a place other than that suited to the house, except the water-ditch for a woman in confinement till the end of ten days (from delivery).

III/8/7: In case of transgression of that, the lowest fine for violence (shall be imposed).

III/8/9: He should cause to be made a deep-flowing water-course or one falling in a cascade, three *padas* away (from a neighbour's wall) or one *aratni* and a half (away).

III/8/10: In case of transgression of that, the fine is fifty-four *paṇas*.

III/8/11: He should cause to be made a place for carts and quadrupeds, a fire-place, a place for the large water-jar, the grinding mill or the pounding machine, one *pada* away or one *aratni* (from a neighbour's wall).

III/8/12: In case of transgression of that, the fine is twenty-four *paṇas*.

III/8/13: Between all two structures or two projecting rooms, (there is to be) an open lane one *kiṣku* (wide) or three *padas*.

III/8/14: Between them, the distance between the eaves of roofs (is to be) four *aṅgulas*, or one may over-lay the other.

III/8/15: He should cause to be made a side-door in the intervening lane, measuring one *kiṣku*, for making repairs to what is damaged, not (allowing) crowding.

III/8/16: For light, he should cause a small window to be made high up.

III/8/19: And he should cause that part above the verandah which requires protection, to be covered by matting, or a wall touching (the roof), for fear of damage by rain.

The above specifications are surprising as Kauṭilya takes into consideration all aspects necessary for perfect harmony in dwelling places of the citizens.

Kauṭilya prescribes various fines and other punitive measures for polluting the environment by throwing dirt on the roads and highways or voiding urine and faeces at public places.

II/36/26: For throwing dirt on the road the fine shall be one eighth (of a *paṇa*), for blocking it with muddy water, one quarter.

II/36/27: On the royal highway, (the fines shall be) double.

II/36/28: Fines for voiding faeces in a holy place, in a place for water, in a temple and in royal property are one *paṇa* rising successively by one *paṇa*, half these for passing urine.

But Kauṭilya was wise enough to realize that sometimes people are compelled to commit the above things due to illness or similar reason. In that case the miscreant is exempted from fines.

To quote:

II/36/29: If (these are) due to medicine, illness or fear, (the persons are) not to be fined.

Throwing carcasses or dead bodies at public places in the city are punishable by fines.

To quote:

II/36/30: For throwing the dead body of a cat, a dog, a ichneumon or a serpent inside the city, the fine shall be three *paṇas*; for throwing the dead body of a donkey, a camel, a mule, a horse or cattle, six *paṇas*; for a human corpse, fifty *paṇas*.

The dead bodies are to be cremated at cremation grounds only. Otherwise the offender will have to pay fines.

To quote:

II/36/33: For depositing and burning (a corpse) elsewhere than in a cremation ground, the fine (shall be) twelve *paṇas*.

Kauṭilya also prescribes that every one should be careful about preserving common property and bio-diversity. Otherwise he would be fined.

To quote:

IV/10/4: In case of theft of deer or objects from deer-parks or produce-forests, (there shall be) a fine of one hundred *paṇas*.

IV/10/5: In case of theft of deer or birds (intended) for show or pleasure or in case of killing these, the fine shall be double.

No one should do anything to have harmful external effects on cultivation, irrigation system and other properties of other persons. Violators of this rule would be punished with fines. In case of setting fire to properties of others or common property, or bursting a dam containing water, the punishment is death-sentence.

To quote:

III/9/27: In case of damage to the ploughing or seeds in another's field by the use of a reservoir, channels or a field under water, they shall pay compensation in accordance with the damage.

III/9/28: In case of mutual damage to fields under water, parks and embankments, the fine (shall be) double the damage.

III/9/29: A tank on a lower level, constructed afterwards, shall not flood with water a field watered by a tank on a higher level.

III/9/30: A (tank) constructed on a higher level shall not prevent the flooding with water of a lower tank, except when its use has ceased for three years.

III/9/31: For transgression of that, (the punishment shall be) the lowest fine for violence and the emptying of the tank.

III/10/5: For encroaching on a path for small animals or men the fine is twelve *paṇas*; on a path for large animals twenty-four *paṇas*, on a road for elephants or fields fifty-four *paṇas*, on a road to a dike or a forest one hundred and six, on a road to a cremation ground or a village two hundred, on a road in a *droṇamukha* five hundred, on a road in a *sthānīya*, the countryside or pasture land, one thousand.

III/10/6: In case of reducing the size of these (roads), the fines are one-quarter of the fines (mentioned).

III/10/7: In case of ploughing (on them, the fines are) as prescribed.

IV/11/17: For one breaking a dam holding water, drowning in water at the same spot (shall be the punishment), the highest fine for violence if it was without water, the middle if it was in ruins and abandoned.

IV/11/20: He shall cause to be burnt in fire one who sets on fire a pasture, a field, a threshing ground, a house, a produce-forest or an elephant forest.

Damage to environment may also be caused by natural hazards. All of them cannot be prevented by human material endeavours, but we may prevent some of them by our knowledge of science and coherent efforts. Kauṭilya's prescription for disaster management is worth noting, particularly the anticipation of disasters and prior preparation for preventing them as far as possible. First he classifies the disasters caused by nature.

To quote:

IV/3/1: There are eight great calamities of a divine origin: fire, floods, disease, famine, rats, wild animals, serpents and evil spirits.

IV/3/2: From them he should protect the country.

Some of the important measures as prescribed by Kauṭilya to prevent natural hazards are discussed below:

Prevention of Natural Hazards

Fire Hazards

The responsibility of controlling hazards from fire and devising rules for the citizens so as to minimize hazards from fire, lies with the City Superintendent.

To quote:

IV/3/4: Prevention of fire is explained in 'Rules for the City Superintendent' and in connection with royal possessions in 'Rules for the Royal Residence'.

Remedies against fire in residential areas and punitive measures against violators of fire-prevention rules are prescribed in the following *ślokas*.

II/36/15: And (citizens shall take) steps against (an outbreak of) fire in summer.

II/36/16: In the two middle quarters of the day, one-eighth (of a *paṇa*) is the fine for (kindling) fire.

II/36/17: Or they should do their cooking outside (the house).

II/36/18: One quarter (of a *paṇa* is the fine) for not providing five jars, also a big jar, a trough, a ladder, an axe, a winnowing-basket, a hook, a 'hair-seizer' and a skin-bag.

II/36/23: For the owner, not running to save the house on fire, the fine (shall be) twelve *paṇas*, six *paṇas* for a tenant.

II/36/24: In case of (houses) catching fire through negligence, the fine (shall be) fifty-four *paṇas*.

The role of the City Superintendent as regards fire prevention is described in the following *ślokas*.

II/36/19: The (City Superintendent) should remove things covered with grass or matting.

II/36/20: He shall make those who live by (the use of) fire reside in one locality.

II/36/22: Collections of water-jars should be placed in thousands on roads and at cross-roads, gates and in royal precincts.

Flood Hazards

In the following *ślokas*, Kauṭilya prescribes measures for prevention of hazards from flood-situations.

IV/3/6: In the rainy season, villages situated near water should live away from the level of the floods.

IV/3/7: And they should keep a collection of wooden planks, bamboos and boats.

Kauṭilya also emphasizes on mass-participation in rescue works. This is done by both moral suasion and legal measures.

To quote:

IV/3/8: They should rescue a (person) being carried away (by the flood) by means of gourds, skin-bags, canoes, tree-stems and rope-braids.

IV/3/9: For those who do not go to the rescue, the fine is twelve *paṇas*, except in the case of those without canoes.

Famine Hazards

The role of the state in famine management, as prescribed by Kauṭilya, is noteworthy. The ruler should have prior preparation for anticipated famines so that he is not caught napping. When the disaster actually occurs, he should take quick measures so as to minimize the harmful effects on the masses. The most interesting aspect in these prescriptions is that the ruler should relinquish if he fails to handle the famine situation.

To quote:

IV/3/17: During a famine, the king should make a store of seeds and food-stuffs and show favour (to the subjects), or (institute) the building of forts or water works with the grant of food, or share (his) provisions (with them), or entrust the country (to another king).

Help of friendly foreign governments may also be sought if it is not possible to manage disaster by the efforts of the government of the affected country alone.

To quote:

IV/3/18: Or, he should seek shelter with allies, or cause a reduction or shifting (of the population).

In fact, ecological and environmental awareness of Kauṭilya can be found in almost all the chapters. It is clear from the above discussion that Kauṭilya was much concerned about matters pertaining to the preservation of environment and ecology. To this end he prescribed various rules and also the punitive measures for violation of such rules. Like Manu, Kauṭilya also had a holistic approach towards environment and ecology as he considered them to be integral parts of human living.

Relevance for Modern India

As a follow-up of the Stockholm International Conference on Environment in 1972 (mentioned at the beginning of this chapter), several international agencies were formed for the protection of environment and ecology of the planet Earth. Mention-worthy among them are:

1. Convention on International Trade in Endangered Species (CITES)
2. Environmental Protection Agency (EPA)
3. United Nations Environment Program (UNEP)
4. South Asia Cooperative Environment Program (SACEP)

This wave of environment awareness also encouraged the Government of India to pass various Acts to protect environment and ecology. Noted among these Acts are:

1. Water (Prevention and Control of Pollution) Act, 1974
2. Air (Prevention and Control of Pollution) Act, 1981
3. Environment (Protection) Act, 1986
4. Motor Vehicles Act, 1998

For implementation of the provisions of these Acts, the Central Pollution Control Board at the central level and State Pollution Control Boards at the state levels were formed in 1988. The Department of Environment, Forest and Wild Life was established in 1985. Mention-worthy among the various government agencies and NGOs (Non-Government Organizations) concerning environment protection in India are:

1. Botanical Survey of India
2. Zoological Survey of India
3. National Wasteland Development Board
4. Central Ganga Authority
5. Bombay Natural History Society
6. Central Forestry Commission
7. Department of Non-Conventional Energy Sources
8. Tata Energy Research Institute (Santra, 2001)

One major shortcoming of all these measures (both at the national and at the international level) is that they are mainly *ad-hoc* in nature and lack holistic approach. In fact, these measures are designed to solve specific problems and do not spring from any basic cosmological and holistic view. So, it has become difficult to coordinate and harmonize various types of activities and agencies designed to protect environment and ecology. These approaches may solve some specific problems pertaining to environment and ecology but would fail to remove the basic cause (which lies in our world outlook and view regarding nature and our relationship with it), which leads to the generation of damage to environment and ecology. In this regard we may learn from the two ancient Indian texts discussed above. For example, Manu specifies (in ***ślokas* 1/27** to **1/57**) why we should think ourselves as a part of the harmonious universe and therefore regulate our material activities in accordance with the rules of nature. This approach towards environment and ecology are likely to generate deeper awareness about these matters among the common people so that they will be more willing to spontaneously cooperate within eco-preserving drives of the government or the NGOs. Kauṭilya's detailed specifications point out how every measure towards preservation of ecology and environment are coherently integrated.

It is true that environmental and ecological problems are now more severe and complicated than those at the time of Manu and Kauṭilya. Many aspects of environmental problems were totally absent in those days. However, if we look deeply into the matter we will realize that all man-made environmental and ecological problems arise because of our greed or ignorance that make us commit things contrary to the balance of nature. The root cause of ecological problems is this and therefore is the same for all ages. The essence of Manu's solution is that people should be made aware that they cannot violate the balance of nature because this will recoil on them as they themselves are inalienable from the same nature created by the Supreme.

In Kauṭilya's age, moral preaching was not enough to prevent people from committing eco-damaging activities. So he specifies punitive measures by the state for violating rules intended to maintain environment and ecology. All these approaches differ from the present *ad-hoc* approach in the sense that today we do not go into the essence of the matter. Rather, we treat every problem in isolation and not as the integral part of our living. Another important aspect of Kauṭilya's prescriptions is that he considers rescue of people from disasters a moral obligation of the ruler. He has no moral right to continue ruling if he fails to manage the disasters in the best possible manner. For example, in connection with famine control, Kauṭilya opines that in case it is not possible for the king to manage the disaster in an appropriate manner he must relinquish and entrust the country with another more competent king [see *śloka* **IV/3/17** above]. The modern rulers should learn from this prescription of Kauṭilya.

Thus, we see that the ancient texts may not only help us in solving specific ecological and environmental problems to a large extent, but they also give us deeper insight into the matter, which will help us solve our problems in a more harmonious way.

This is the relevance of the ancient texts like Manusmṛti and Arthaśāstra of Kauṭilya for modern India and, for that matter, the modern world.

Reference

Santra, S.C. (ed.) (2001): *Current Perspective of Environmental Science,* Department of Environmental Science, University of Kalyani, Nadia, West Bengal.

5

Craft Industries

Self-employment through Crafts

In course of industrialization, particularly during the era of liberalization, one of the most serious problems is the problem of increasing unemployment, as modern industries are highly capital intensive. For rapid economic development of the country, modern industries with sophisticated foreign technologies need to be built up. At the same time, it is to be seen that adequate employment opportunities are generated for the job-seekers, whose number is increasing rapidly with growth of population. Formal sector led by modern industries, as we have already mentioned, is incapable of handling the employment aspect. So, the informal sector also has to shoulder the major burden of job creation for the rising job-seekers. The agricultural sector has already been saturated as regards providing employment. In fact, it is burdened with the problem of surplus manpower (the so-called 'disguised unemployment'). So, it is an urgent necessity to find out a safety net for the job seekers. The handicraft industries are likely to play a major role in this regard. But, this sector is burdened with various problems, most of which have remained unresolved in spite of efforts by the Government of India since the First Five-Year Plan.

In ancient India, these craft industries were highly developed and efficient. So, the question arises whether we can learn from the ancient texts as regards reviving the craft industries and making them capable of creating enough jobs. The most mention-worthy thing in this regard is that job creation through the crafts automatically takes place if the crafts prosper without any subsidy or government reservation (which is an undesirable aspect of the present policy regarding the crafts in India). In ancient India, this was possible because of the high quality of products of the crafts.

Nowadays, many cheap goods are produced by the large-scale modern industries, but the craft products dependent on human skill cannot be imitated by modern industries. These products are likely to command a large market if the quality of products is ensured, but here the craft industries in India today fail. Because of the low quality of products the craft industries require government reservation since their substandard products cannot be sold unless the government departments buy them or they gain monopoly power through government reservation. This policy of generating employment through the crafts is at the cost of the consumers, which is not at all desirable. So, we need to study how the quality of products was ensured in ancient India. This was mainly ensured by strict government regulations on the guilds regarding quality of products of the craft industries. We shall discuss these matters in the following but before going into the prescriptions in the ancient Indian texts regarding the crafts, let us have a glimpse of the history (origin, evolution and decline) of the craft industries in India.

History

A large number of highly efficient crafts, many of which originated as early as the Vedic period, flourished in ancient India, especially since 700 B.C. M.A. Buch cites the existence of the following crafts during this period: cotton, silk and woolen textiles; perfumes; glass works and mirrors; umbrellas; shoes and other leather goods; wood works; ivory works; mining and metallurgy (gold, silver, iron, tin, zinc, copper, lead), ornaments etc. (Buch, 1979: 116-97). The artisans had acquired remarkable skill in each branch of craft because of helpful socio-economic and political set up (*ibid.:* 202-36).

Buch mentions the following conditions conducive to this situation:

(i) Autonomy and dignity of labour.

(ii) High position of labour in society.

(iii) The Indian economic system that relied more on status than on contract, was quite favourable to artistic production.

(iv) Absence of inequality.

(v) Patronage of the state.

(vi) The caste system, the guild and the village community were institutions, which were in many ways favourable to the creation and conservation of true art.

(vii) The guilds used to maintain quality of products.

(viii) Village community and land tenure system led to wonderful continuity and unity of ancient Indian arts and crafts.

(ix) Genius for imitation of the artisans.

(x) Systematic technical training from childhood.

(xi) Governing influence of religious ethics.

(xii) Healthy home atmosphere.

Crafts of ancient India were highly organized under strong guilds (*sreṇīs*), which had evolved since the Vedic times. Almost every important craft or occupation in a locality used to form a guild. Persons belonging to each craft used to acquire the profession on the basis of heredity. They used to settle down in a well defined region and were organized in guilds under a *Jeṭṭhaka* or *Pamukha*. The guilds possessed both executive and judicial power and were entitled to arbitrate between its members through executive officers. Some guilds worked as banks and used to receive permanent deposits. Sometimes, a number of guilds got united to form a federation presided over by a *Bhāṇḍagārika* (Mookerji, 1980: 601-02).

Panikkar opines that guilds used to enjoy great economic and political power (Panikkar, 1966: 36).

The British rule in India, particularly since the middle of the 19th century, gave a deadly blow to the major crafts in India. The kings and the Noble Class, with their refined tastes for high quality craft products, were degenerated, and the guild system got disintegrated under the administrative reorganization of the British rulers. The newly emerging factory industries in Britain sought a reliable and secure market for their products in India. This necessitated deliberate destruction of the craft industries like the cotton textiles, which were likely to out-compete the British industries producing the same type of products at that time (Gadgil, 1973: 33-36).

In this process, the major crafts like the cotton, woolen and silk textiles were affected adversely but a host of crafts producing artistic goods, which could not be produced in modern factories, remained almost unaffected. But the plight of the artisans became precarious because of poverty, exploitation by the middlemen and moneylenders, and erosion of market for quality products because of the degeneration of the Noble Class with refined tastes. Many artisans left their hereditary profession and sought employment elsewhere. In recent years, however, there has been a sign of revival of many of the crafts because of an expanding foreign market. This sector has also opened up possibilities of generating considerable employment opportunities.

Now, let us look into the information on craft industries obtained from the Manusmṛti and Arthaśāstra of Kauṭilya, and examine if they are of any help in the process of revival of the craft industries in India.

Manusmṛti

Manu only briefly mentions that crafts are to be the professions of the *Śūdra*, as in the following *ślokas*:

10/99: But a *Śūdra*, being unable to find service with the twice-born and threatened with the loss of his sons and wife (through hunger), may maintain himself by handicrafts.

10/100: (Let him follow) those mechanical occupations and those various practical arts by following which the twice-born are (best) served.

Arthaśāstra

There are innumerable mentions of the state-sector craft industries in the Arthaśāstra of Kauṭilya. Some of the relevant extracts are quoted below:

II/12/1: The Director of Mines, being conversant with the science of (metal) veins in the earth and metallurgy, the art of smelting and the art of colouring gems, or having the assistance of experts in these, and fully equipped with workmen skilled in the work and with implements, should inspect an old mine by the marks of dross, crucibles, coal and ashes, or a new mine, where there are ores in the earth, in rocks or in liquid form, with excessive colour and heaviness and with a strong smell and taste.

II/12/18: What is produced from ores, he should put to use in factories for the respective metals.

II/12/23: The Director of Metals should establish factories for copper, lead, tin, *vaikṛntaka*, brass, steel, bronze, bell-metal and iron, also (establish) trade in metalware.

II/12/24: The Mint Master should cause to be minted silver coins ....

II/12/27: The Superintendent of Mines should establish factories for (articles of) conch-shells, diamonds, gems, pearls, corals and caustics as well as commerce in them.

II/13/37: Setting, stringing, and minor work, these are ways of working (in gold).

II/13/38: Setting is the fixing of binding and so on.

II/13/39: Stringing is weaving in threads and so on.

II/13/40: (Making) a solid article, a hollow article or one with beads and so on is minor work.

II/14/1: The Goldsmith should cause the gold and silver work of the citizens and the country people to be carried out by workshop artisans.

II/17/1: The Director of Forest Produce should cause forest produce to be brought in by guards in the produce forests.

II/17/2: And he should start factories for forest produce.

II/17/15: Vessels made of split bamboo-cane and of clay

II/17/16: Charcoal, husks and ashes; enclosures for deer, beasts, birds and wild animals and enclosures for fuel and grass.

II/17/17: Separate factories making all kinds of goods should be erected, outside as well as inside, by the Director of Forest Produce, for ensuring livelihood and protection of the city.

II/18/1: The Superintendent of the Armoury should cause to be made machines for use in battles, for the defence of forts and for assault on the enemies' cities, also weapons, armours and accoutrements by artisans and artists expert in those lines, producing goods with an agreement as to the amount of work, time allowed and wages, and should store them in places suitable for each.

II/19/1: The Superintendent of Standardization should cause factories to be established for the manufacture of standard weights and measures.

II/23/1: The Superintendent of Yarns should cause trade to be carried out in yarns, armours, cloth and ropes through men expert in the work.

II/23/2: He should get yarn spun out of wool, bark-fibres, cotton, silk-cotton, hemp and flax, through widows, crippled women, maidens, women who have left their homes and women paying off their fine by personal labour, through mothers of courtesans, through old female slaves of the king and through female slaves of temples whose service of the gods has ceased.

II/23/9: He should bring about the production of varieties of cloth, bed-sheets and coverings.

II/23/10: And he should start factories for armours by artisans and craftsmen expert in the line.

II/23/18: And he should cause articles, such as straps and others to be manufactured.

II/23/19: He should cause ropes to be made of yarn and fibres, (and) thongs of canes and bamboos, as trappings for war and bindings for vehicles and draught-animals.

II/33/1: The (duty of the) Superintendent of Chariots is explained by (that of) the Superintendent of Horses.

II/33/2: He should establish factories for (the manufacture of) chariots.

The above *ślokas* reveal that innumerable commodities were produced in the craft industries in those days.

Besides these prescriptions for state sector craft products, there are mentions of thousands of commodities (particularly in **Book II, Chapters 11** and **15**), which indicate the range and variety of craft products in those days. Kauṭilya also mentions the craft guilds in **Book IV, Chapter 1**.

Relevant Extracts from Book II, Chapter 11 of Arthaśāstra

II/11/2: That from the Tāmraparṇī, that from Pāṇḍyaka-vāṭa, that from the Pāśikā, that from the Kulā, that from the Cūrṇī, that from (Mt.) Mahendra, that from the Kardamā, that from the Srotasī, that from the Lake, and that from the Himavat, these are pearls.

II/11/28: Gems come from Koṭi, from the Mālā and from beyond the sea.

II/11/37: Diamonds come from Sabhārāṣṭra, from Tajjamārāṣṭra, from Kāstīrarāṣṭra, from (Mt.) Śrīkaṭanaka, from (Mt.) Maṇimanta and from Indravāna.

II/11/42: The Coral from Alakananda and from Vivarṇa.

II/11/43: Sandalwood from Sātana is red and has the smell of the earth.

II/11/44: That from Gośīrṣa is blackish red and smells like fish.

II/11/45: The sandalwood from Hari is of the colour of the parrot's feather and has the smell of a mango, also that from the Tṛṇasā.

II/11/46: That from Grāmeru is red or red-black and has the smell of goat's urine.

II/11/47: That from Devasabhā is red and has the smell of a lotus, also that from Jāpa.

II/11/48: That from Joṅga is red or red-black and smooth, also that from Turūpa.

II/11/49: That from the Mālā is whitish red.

II/11/50: *Kucandana* is rough, black like aloe or red or reddish black.

II/11/51: That from Kāla mountain is reddish-black or of the colour of saffron.

II/11/52: That from the Kośāgāra mountain is black or black-variegated.

II/11/53: That from the Śītodakā has the lustre of the lotus or is black and smooth.

II/11/54: That from Nāga mountain is rough or of the colour of moss.

II/11/55: That from Śākala is brown.

II/11/57: Aloe from Joṅga is black, black-variegated or variegated with round spots.

II/11/58: That from Doṅga is dark.

II/11/61: *Tailaparṇika* (incense) from Aśokagrāma has the colour of flesh and the fragrance of a lotus.

II/11/62: That from Joṅga is reddish yellow and has the fragrance of a blue lotus or the smell of cow's urine.

II/11/63: That from Grāmeru is smooth and has the smell of cow's urine.

II/11/64: That from Suvarṇakuḍya is reddish yellow and has the smell of the citron fruit.

II/11/65: That from Pūrṇakadvīpa has the fragrance of a lotus or the smell of butter.

II/11/66: *Bhadraśriya* from beyond the Lauhityā is of the colour of the *jātī*-flower.

II/11/67: That from Antaravatī is of the colour of *uśīra*.

II/11/69: *Kāleyaka* from Suvarṇabhūmi is smooth and yellow.

II/11/70: That from the northern mountain is reddish yellow.

II/11/77: The *bisī* and the *mahābisī* come from Dvādaśagrāma.

II/11/81: The *śyāmikā*, the *kālikā*, the *kadalī*, the *candrottarā* and the *śākulā* are produced in Āroha.

II/11/88: The *sāmūra*, the *chīnasī*, and the *sāmūlī* come from Bāhlava.

II/11/92: The *sātinā*, the *nalatūlā*, and the *vṛttapuchhā* are from Odra.

II/11/100: ….the *apasāraka* which keeps off rain, – that is (woolen cloth) from Nepāla.

II/11/102: The *dukūla* from the Vaṅgas is white and smooth.

II/11/103: That from the Puṇḍras is dark and smooth like a gem.

II/11/104: That from Suvarṇakuḍya is of the colour of the sun, with gem-smooth water-weave, with a uniform weave and with a mixed weave.

II/11/106: By that is explained the *Kṣauma* from Kāśī and Puṇḍras.

II/11/107: The *patrorṇā*-silk comes from the Magadhas, the Puṇḍras and Suvarṇakuḍya.

II/11/114: By that are explained the silk and silk-cloth from the land of Cīna.

II/11/115: Cotton fabrics from Madhurā, the Aparāntas, the Kaliṅgas, Kāśī, the Vaṅgas, the Vatsas and the Mahiṣas, are best.

The above extracts show the varieties of high quality craft products produced in ancient India. This high quality was the cornerstone of success for the crafts in those days. This was possible because of the existence of the guilds which maintained a strict surveillance over the quality at all stages of production beginning from the raw materials. They also helped the individual artisans to market their products. Thus employment was automatically generated without any reservation for the crafts. Kauṭilya was also aware that the guilds themselves may acquire monopoly power and thereby destroy competition. So, state control over the guilds and artisans was necessary in order to protect the interests of the consumer.

To quote:

IV/1/65: In this manner the (king) should prevent thieves who are not known as thieves such as traders, artisans, actors, mendicants, jugglers and others from oppressing the country.

Importance and role of the guilds in ensuring quality of raw materials and final products is described in the following *ślokas*.

IV/1/2: Employers of artisans capable of making good an article, those good at entrusting materials, (and) artisans working with their own capital should accept entrusted material with the guarantee of the guild.

IV/1/3: In case of death, the guild shall be responsible for the entrusted material.

The regulations for the artisans in general are described in the following *ślokas*.

IV/1/4: And they shall carry out the work with the place, time and (nature of the) work stipulated, without stipulation as to place or time if the nature of the work can be pointed out (as the reason).

IV/1/5: For exceeding the time limit, (there shall be) a reduction in the wage by one quarter and double that as fine.

IV/1/6: They shall be liable for what is lost or destroyed except in case of deterioration or a sudden calamity.

IV/1/7: For carrying out a work otherwise than as ordered, (there shall be) loss of wage and double that as fine.

Regulations Regarding Quality, Wages and Fines (in case of violation)

Weavers

IV/1/8: Weavers shall increase yarn to the extent of eleven (*palas*) from ten.

IV/1/9: For diminution in increase, the fine shall be double the diminution.

IV/1/10: The wage for weaving (shall be equal to) the value of the yarn, one and a half times in the case of *kṣauma* and *kauśeya*, double in the case of *patrorṇā*, blankets and *dukūla*.

IV/1/11: For shortness in measure, (there shall be) a reduction in wage equal to (the value of) the short measure and double that as fine, for short weight the fine (shall be) four times the deficiency, for change of yarn (the fine shall be) double its value.

IV/1/13: In one *tulā* of wool, a reduction in carding to the extent of five *palas* (is allowed), and (the same amount of) reduction in the hair (when carded).

Washermen

IV/1/14: Washermen shall wash garments on wooden boards or smooth slabs of stone.

IV/1/15: Those washing on anything else shall pay for damage to garments and a fine of six *paṇas*.

IV/1/16: (Washermen) wearing a garment other than one marked with the sign of the club shall pay a fine of three *paṇas*.

IV/1/17: For selling, hiring out or pledging the garments of others the fine shall be twelve *paṇas*, for change of garments (the fine shall be) double the price and the return of the garment.

IV/1/18: They shall return a garment, which is white like a bud, which is cleansed on a slab of stone, which has the colour of washed yarn, and which is bleached white, after one day increased successively by one day.

IV/1/19: One with a light red colour (may be returned) after five days, one dyed blue after six days, a precious garment dyed in (saffron) flower, lac-juice or *mañjiṣṭhā* the treatment of which is arduous and which has to be worked upon with great care, after seven days.

IV/1/20: After that they shall lose their wage.

IV/1/21: In cases of dispute concerning dyeing, trustworthy experts shall fix the wage.

IV/1/22: For the most precious (garments) the wage (shall be) one *paṇa*, for middling one half, for lowest one-quarter, for rough (garments) one *māṣaka* or two *māṣakas*, double for dyed (garments).

IV/1/23: At the first washing there is a loss of one-fourth (of the value of the garment), at the second of one-fifth.

IV/1/24: By that are explained later (losses in value).

Tailors

Rules for the tailors are the same as specified for the weavers above.

To quote:

IV/1/25: By washermen are explained tailors.

IV/1/26: For goldsmiths purchasing silver (or) gold in the same form from the hands of a disreputable person without informing (state officers) the fine is twenty *paṇas*, if in a changed form twenty-four *paṇas*, if from the hands of a thief forty-eight *paṇas*.

IV/1/27: In cases of purchase at a low price in secret or what is changed in appearance there shall be the punishment for theft, also in case of deceit in the article manufactured.

IV/1/28: For (the goldsmith) stealing one *māṣaka* from one *suvarṇa* (of gold) the fine shall be two hundred *paṇas*, for stealing one *māṣaka* from one *dharaṇa* of silver twelve *paṇas*.

IV/1/29: By that are explained higher (values).

IV/1/30: For one securing an (artificial) enhancement of colour or practising removal or mixture (with base metals), the fine shall be five hundred *paṇas*.

IV/1/31: In case of fraud in connection with these two (metals), he shall treat it as (a case of) removal of colour.

IV/1/32: One *māṣaka* is the wage for one *dharaṇa* of silver, one-eighth part (of a *paṇa*) for one *suvarṇa* (of gold).

IV/1/33: In accordance with special skill, the wage may be increased to double.

IV/1/34: By that are explained further rates.

In this **Book IV, Chapter 1, *ślokas* 35-64**, there are innumerable such guidelines and regulations for the artisans of base-metal like copper, iron, steel, bell-metal, *vaikṛntaka*, brass and lead, for the artisans making and examining coins, for the physicians, for the actors, the mendicants, wandering minstrels etc.

Relevance for Modern India

The fresh air of liberalism and economic freedom in the global scenario encouraged India, which was languishing in the quagmire of economic stagnation, to adopt the New Economic Policy (NEP) in June 1991. Liberalization, privatization and globalization (LPG) was the catchword for the NEP. Under the new set up a number of stabilization measures (with reforms of trade, fiscal and industrial policies), were undertaken. The major thrust was on improvement of competitive efficiency in the industrial sector with the assistance of foreign capital and technology. Sixteen years have elapsed since the adoption of the Structural Adjustment Programme (SAP), an integral part of NEP. Various criticisms have been leveled against it, with the increasing unemployment, which is an unavoidable consequence of the reform measures, being the most important one.

The annual average growth rate of employment in the organized industrial sector declined from 1.27 per cent over 1983-94 to only 0.54 per cent over 1994-2000. This indicates an increase in overall unemployment during the SAP period unless the loss in employment in the organized industrial sector is compensated by the growth of employment in other sectors. But available data reveal that the performance of the primary sector, tertiary sector and the unorganized industrial sector taken together also shows a declining rate of employment during this period with the annual growth rate declining from 2.04 per cent during 1993-94 to 0.98 per cent during 1994-2000 (Dutt, 2001: 464-71).

Thus, it is seen that, in spite of achievements in various fields, effect of the SAP on employment in India has been highly alarming. So it is an urgent necessity to find out a 'Safety-Net' to absorb the unemployed persons resulting from the measures under the SAP. In this respect the craft industries can play an important role. These industries are highly labour-intensive as they require small capital investment and depend on indigenous skill. The prospect of expansion of market for these industries, both internal and foreign, has increased considerably in recent years. Moreover, the export performance of these industries in recent years has made them one of the major sources of export earning. Exports of craft products as a percentage of total exports of India increased from 4.78 per cent in 1970-71 to 18.94 per cent in 1990-91[1] and thereafter the programme slumped down and in

2002-03 it was 19.3 per cent. These industries however, are afflicted with various problems. Unless proper measures are adopted to remove these problems, these industries would not be able to play their proper role in solving the unemployment problem and contributing substantially to foreign earnings of our country.

Existing Government Policy

Since the First Five-Year Plan (1951-56), the Government of India has attached great importance to the craft industries for employment and income generation in the rural sector. In November 1952, the All India Handicrafts Board was set up to advice the government on the problems of the crafts industries. The Board was reconstituted as the All India Handlooms and Handicrafts Board (AIHHB) in July 1981, to render joint advice on handlooms as well as handicrafts. The Directorate of Industry and the Development Corporation for Handicrafts, under the state governments, undertake to help in production and creation of domestic market for the handicrafts. The major Central Government organizations established for the revival of the craft industries in India are the following:

1. Handicrafts and Handlooms Export Corporation.
2. Central Cottage Industries Emporium.
3. North-Eastern Handicrafts and Handlooms Development Corporation.
4. Four Regional Design and Technical Development Centers.
5. A Crafts Museum in New Delhi.
6. 39 Marketing and Service Extension Centres.
7. Training Centres for Different Crafts.
8. 24 Common Facility Centres.
9. 25 Raw Material Depots (Kathuria, 1988).

Unfortunately, these efforts of the government turned out to be quite inadequate for the revival of the craft industries and the situation has changed very little during the last two decades. After adoption of the NEP, the industrial policy of the Government of India has laid more emphasis on the achievement of a high growth rate of the organized industrial sector, and the policy regarding the Handicrafts has remained incoherent in spite of increasing contribution of this sector to export earnings and employment generation (*ibid.:* 130).

On the basis of the above, analysis the following observations may be made:

(i) Revival of handicrafts in India to generate adequate employment opportunities, depends mainly on exports.

(ii) Export prospect of the existing export oriented crafts may soon be saturated.

(iii) Revival of crafts in India with expansion of exports is fraught with a number of serious problems.

(iv) The private sector cannot be relied upon for their revival.

(v) Role of government institutions, too, is questionable.

The most pertinent question as regards revival of the crafts is the maintenance of quality of the products, which also requires assured supply of high-quality raw materials. All these tasks were accomplished in ancient India by the craft guilds.

So, one way out is to organize the crafts in India at present under cooperatives on the lines of the ancient guilds with the following tasks:

(i) Maintenance of skill of the artisans and quality of the products.

(ii) Arrangement of easy credit facilities for the artisans from banks and other financial institutions.

(iii) Sales promotion in internal and foreign markets.

(iv) Technology upgradation.

(v) Redesigning to meet needs of the modern buyers.

(vi) Collection of products from the small artisans, arrangements for storing and exporting.

One strong objection against cooperatives is that they will lead to monopoly and reduce competitiveness. But many opine that there is no trade-off between cooperation and competition. In ancient times there was competition among the guilds, which was one of the factors that compelled each of them to be conscious about maintaining the quality of its product. Otherwise, there was the danger that products of other guilds (may be of other localities), would capture the market. So it would be a correct policy to encourage formation of cooperatives along with competition among them. But, to ensure quality and competition, it is also necessary to do away with the present system of subsidy and reservation for the crafts. In ancient India, there was no policy to generate employment through reservation. Reservation and subsidies lead to inefficiency and therefore development of crafts by these policies is not sustainable.

Besides cooperatives, self-employment may also be generated through crafts by providing bank loans and training facilities by experts to the unemployed who are desirous of establishing craft industries. Some provisions to make such projects successful could be providing loans, ensuring marketing facilities and above all, strictly maintaining quality of products. Quality specifications as found in Kautilya's treatise in detail is an urgent necessity for framing rules regarding maintenance of quality of products and activities of the artisans (whether belonging to co-operatives or functioning as free self-employed businessmen). We also learn from Arthaśāstra of Kauṭilya that the cooperatives should be strictly regulated by the state as regards quality and other consumer services.

Forming a cooperative system with these tasks is the most effective method for revival of the crafts in India, and in this regard the rules and guidelines in ancient texts (especially Arthaśāstra of Kauṭilya) about the craft industries and craft-guilds may be of considerable help.

In brief, the lessons for modern India from the ancient Indian texts as regards craft industries are:

(i) Development of crafts under subsidies and reservation is not sustainable and should therefore be done away with.

(ii) Formation of cooperatives in line with ancient craft-guilds may be encouraged.

(iii) Encouragement to self-employment through craft industries by provision of bank loans, training facilities by experts and marketing facilities.

(iv) The state should regulate the cooperatives to ensure healthy competition.

(v) Quality of products and nature of activities of the artisans are to be rigidly specified and maintained by strict state laws as prescribed by Kauṭilya.

Notes

1. Calculated from Table 7.3(A), S-84, 85 *Economic Survey*, 2002-03.
2. *Statistical Outline of India*, Tata, p. 86.

References

Buch, M.A. (1979): *Economic Life in Ancient India*, R.S. Publishing House, Allahabad.

Dutt, R. (2001): "Economic Liberalisation and its Implications for Employment in India" in the *Conference Volume*, 84th Annual Conference of the Indian Economic Association, Vellore, Tamil Nadu.

Gadgil, D.R. (1973): *Industrial Evolution in India in Recent Times*, Oxford University Press, Delhi.

Government of India: Economic Survey, 2002-03.

Kathuria, S. (1988): *Indian Handicraft Exports: Constraints and Prospects*, Tata McGraw Hill Publishing Co. Ltd., New Delhi.

Mookerji, R.K. (1980): "Economic Conditions" in Majumdar, R.C. (ed.), *The History and Culture of Indian People, Vol.II*, Bharatiya Vidya Bhawan, Bombay.

Panikkar, K.M. (1960): *A Survey of Indian History*, Asia Publishing House, Bombay.

Statistical Outline of India 2003-2004, Tata Services Limited, Mumbai.

6

Role of the State Sector

Efficient State Sector only for Selected Areas

After independence the Indian economy laid great emphasis on state sector economic activities and, in course of time, there emerged a vast and all-comprehensive state sector in India. But soon criticisms started being levelled at the state sector mainly on the grounds of huge losses, inefficiency, corruption etc. The necessity of such an all-comprehensive state sector was also questioned from a pure theoretical ground. It this chapter, we shall see what lessons we can have in this regard from the two ancient Indian texts, viz., Manusmṛti and Arthaśāstra of Kauṭilya.

Manusmṛti

We get very little information as regards the state sector from Manusmṛti. From the following *śloka*, however, we learn that the king used to have monopoly (of exporṭ) over certain goods:

8/399: Let the king confiscate the whole property of (a trader) who out of greed exports goods of which the king has a monopoly or (the export of which is) forbidden.

This is the only *śloka* in Manusmṛti that mentions state sector. It may be that state sector economic activities were not favoured by this text but Manu prescribes various benevolent activities for the state and opines that the king should behave like a father to his subjects.

To quote:

7/80: He should collect annual rent from his kingdom through officers. In all worldly matters he should stick to the Vedas and should behave towards the people as a father.

8/172: By taking his due, by preventing the confusion of the castes (*varṇa*), and by protecting the weak, the power of the king grows, and he prospers in this (world) and after death.

The above *ślokas* point out the basic approach of the state towards welfare of the subjects. There are also brief mentions of some specific favours for the weaker sections of the community as in the following *ślokas*:

8/28: In like manner care must be taken of barren women, of those who have no sons, of those whose family is extinct, of wives and widows faithful to their lords, and of women afflicted with diseases.

8/407: But a woman who has been pregnant two months or more, an ascetic, a hermit in the forest, and *Brāhmaṇa* who are students of the Veda, shall not be made to pay toll at a ferry.

Arthaśāstra

Description of a vast state sector is mainly given in the **Book II** of Arthaśāstra of Kauṭilya. The relevant segments are given below:

The state should have monopoly power over most of the natural animal products and plant products.

To quote:

II/1/24: The ownership of the fish, ducks, and green vegetables in the irrigation works should go to the king.

It may also be presumed that the state had ownership of most of the mines producing metallic ores and controlling power over trade in these products.

To quote:

II/12/18: (see **Chapter 4** above)

II/12/19: He should establish trade in manufactured goods in a single place, and (lay down) a penalty for those who manufacture, purchase or sell elsewhere.

The state also leased out mines to private businessmen. But in this respect the best mines were to be explored by the state itself and the difficult ones to be leased out to private party.

To quote:

II/12/22: He should let for part-share or on lease a mine that is burden-some in point of expenses or working; a light one, he should work himself.

The following *śloka* indicates monopoly power of the state over salt mines. But here also some salt mines were leased out to private parties in exchange for rent and surcharges:

To quote:

II/12/28: The Salt Commissioner should collect at the proper time the share of salt as released after crystallization as well as the lease-rent, also the price, the inspection fee and the surcharge from the sale.

The state had almost monopoly power over exploration of gold and production of ornaments and other articles by these precious metals.

To quote:

II/13/1: The Superintendent of Gold should cause to be built a workshop with a courtyard having four work-halls without inter-communication (and) with a single door, for the manufacture of gold and silver.

II/13/2: In the middle of the market highway he should establish the Goldsmith, skilled in his profession, of noble birth and trustworthy.

All measuring scales and weights were to be produced by the state.

To quote:

II/14/15: They shall purchase the scales and weights from the Superintendent of Standardization.

The command of the state sector over the economy is also exemplified by the *ślokas*.

II/12/23; II/12/27; II/17/1; II/17/2; II/17/15-17; II/18/1; II/23/1 and **II/33/2** (see **Chapter 4** above).

The above extracts give an elaborate account of the state sector economic activities. It is seen that almost all the goods available in those days were produced in the state sector. The state also used to participate in inland and overseas trade. In certain fields, the state used to enjoy almost exclusive monopoly power. They were: mining, fisheries, transport, production of boats, ships, and vehicles, coins and salt. In these spheres, however, private persons were permitted to operate under certain conditions and under strict state control. The state had exclusive right over all forest and oceanic products.

In other spheres however, private production was permitted. Agricultural commodities were produced in both the private sector and the state sector. It appears that most of the trading (internal and foreign) activities were carried on by private traders.

Thus, a study of Arthaśāstra of Kauṭilya creates the impression that the major part of the national product was produced in the state sector.

For smooth and efficient operation of the state machinery, Kauṭilya divided the vast state sector activities into a large number of departments, each department entrusted to a Superintendent, Director or Departmental Head. The most important departments were: 1. Stores Department; 2. Revenue Administration; 3. Audit and Accounts Department; 4. Treasury; 5. Department of Mines and Factories; 6. Department of Gold; 7. Department of Magazine; 8. Department of Trade and

Commerce; 9. Department of Forests; 10. Armoury; 11. Department for Weights and Measures; 12. Department for Space and Time; 13. Customs Department; 14. Department for Yarns; 15. Department of Agriculture; 16. Department for Spirituous Liquor; 17. Slaughter House; 18. Department for Courtesans; 19. Shipping Department; 20. Department for Cattle; 21. Department for Horses; 22. Department for Elephants; 23. Department for Chariots; 24. Infantry; 25. Army; 26. Department for Passports and Pastureland; 27. Village Administration; 28. Department for Secret Agents; and 29. City Administration.

Various hypotheses have been put forward to explain the prescription of such a vast and all-comprehensive state sector in Arthaśāstra. None of them is, however, fully satisfactory. The important ones are discussed below:

(i) The vast size of the empire necessitated vast amount of revenue. For small states, it was possible to mobilize necessary revenue by taxation alone but for a vast state like the one conceived by Kauṭilya, adequate finance could not be mobilized through taxation alone. So it became necessary to supplement tax revenue by profits from the state sector business and productive activities.

(ii) Private sector productive activities particularly by the craft industries under the guilds, were not adequate to meet the requirements of the society. So it was necessary to undertake productive activities under the state.

(iii) Protection and proper use of natural resources like forests, lakes, rivers, mineral and water resources etc. compelled the state to have exhaustive monopoly over these fields.

(iv) Technological expansion in that period necessitated state intervention and direct participation by the state in productive activities.

However none of these explanations is fully satisfactory. So further research in this regard is an urgent necessity. Two observations, however, about the vast state sector in the Arthaśâstra, can be made on the basis of the existing information:

(a) The concept of a vast state sector was a temporary phenomenon, specifically relevant to the age of the Arthaśāstra, when for the first time India as a single political entity, encompassing a vast geographical area, emerged. We draw this conclusion because this concept is absent in the guidelines prescribed in the major texts in the later periods in ancient India.

(b) In the Arthaśāstra, utmost emphasis was given to the efficiency and profitability of the state sector.

The discussion of the state sector in Kauṭilya's Arthaśāstra would remain incomplete without a glimpse of the Audit and Accounting system by which such vast and varied activities of the state were harmoniously carried on.

Audit and Accounting

Detailed and accurate methods of accounting and auditing, as delineated in Arthaśāstra of Kauṭilya, reminds one of the accounting methods of a highly developed capitalist economy. Some of them are: salaries of all the state employees should be paid promptly, all state orders should be in writing, power and duties of all the state departments should be clearly defined, separate registers should be maintained for every item and accounts should be regularly entered in prescribed registers. Some other relevant aspects are revealed by the following extracts. In **Chapter 7 of Book II** of Arthaśāstra, the functions of the Superintendent of Audit and Accounts are prescribed in the following manner:

II/7/1: The Superintendent should cause the Record Office to be built facing the east or the north, with separate halls, (as) a place for record books.

II/7/2: There he should cause to be entered in the record books: the extent of the number, activity and total (income) of the departments; the amount of increase or decrease in the use of the (various) materials, expenses, excess, surcharge, mixing, place, wages and labourers in connection with factories; the price, the quality, the weight, the measure, the height, the depth and the container in connection with jewels, articles of high value, of low value and forest produce; laws, transactions, customs and fixed rules of regions, villages, castes, families and corporations; the receipt of favours, lands, use, exemptions, and food and wages by those who serve the king; the receipt of jewels and land (and) the receipt of special allowances and (payments for) remedial measures against sudden calamities, by the king and his queens and sons; and payments and receipts in connection with peace and war with allies and enemies.

II/7/3: From that he should hand over in writing the (revenue) estimate, accrued revenue, outstanding revenue, income and expenditure, balance, (the time for) attendance (for audit), (sphere of) activity, customs and fixed rules, to all the departments.

As regards the functions of the officers of different departments pertaining to auditing of the records of the respective departments, Kauṭilya prescribes the following guidelines:

II/7/16: The accounts should come in on Āṣāḍha full moon day.

II/7/17: When the (officers) have come with sealed account books and balances in sealed containers, he should impose restriction in one place, not allowing conversation (among them).

II/7/18: After hearing the totals of income, expenditure and balance, he should cause the balance to be taken away (to the treasury).

II/7/21: For (officers) not coming at the proper time or coming without the account books and balances, the fine shall be one-tenth of the amount due.

II/7/22: And if, when the works officer presents himself, the accounts officer is not ready to audit, the lowest fine for violence (shall be imposed).

II/7/23: In the reverse case, the fine for the works officer (shall be) double.

II/7/24: The high officers should render accounts in full in accordance with their activity, without contradicting themselves.

II/7/25: And among these he who makes a divergent statement or speaks falsely shall pay the highest fine (for violence).

The account books of different departments are to be presented in full before the audit officer in time. In case of delay due to unavoidable circumstances, some concessions in this regard may be made, but up to a certain limit.

To quote:

II/7/26: He should wait for one month, if the (officer) has not brought in the day-to-day accounts.

II/7/27: After the month, the (officer) shall pay a fine of two hundred *paṇas* increased (by that amount) for each succeeding month.

II/7/28: If an (officer) has a little of written balance due (from him), he should wait for five days.

II/7/29: If he brings in the day-to-day accounts after that period, preceded by (delivery of the balance into) the treasury, he should look into (the case) with reference to laws, transactions, customs and fixed rules and by totalling up, (and by looking at) the work actually carried out, by inference and the use of spies.

The guidelines of checking up the accounts by the audit and accounts officer are prescribed in the following *ślokas*:

II/7/30: And he should check (the accounts) for each day, group of five days, fortnight, month, four months and year.

II/7/31: He should check the income with reference to the period, place, time, head of income, source, bringing forward, quantity, the payer, the person causing payment to be made, the recorder and the receiver.

II/7/32: He should check the expenditure with reference to the period, place, time, head (of expenditure), gain, occasion, the thing given, its use and amount, the person who orders, the person who takes out, the person who delivers and the receiver.

II/7/33: He should check the balance with reference to the period, place, time, head, bringing forward, the article, its characteristics, amount, the vessel in which it is deposited and the person guarding it.

The restrictions on the accounts officer and various punitive measures against him, in case he fails to discharge his assigned duties in a proper way, are prescribed in the following *ślokas*:

II/7/34: If, in an affair of the king, the accounts officer is not ready for audit or disregards an order or changes the income and expenditure in a way different from the written order, the lowest fine for violence (shall be imposed).

II/7/35: For one writing down an item (in the accounts) without any order or in a wrong order or in an illegible manner, or twice over, the fine is twelve *paṇas*.

II/7/36: For one writing down the balance (in any of these ways) the fine is double (that).

II/7/39: In case of a false statement, the punishment is that for theft.

II/7/40: If admitted afterwards, (the fine is) double, so also if an item is forgotten and then brought in.

The process of maintaining accounts by the Director of Stores is prescribed in the following *ślokas*.

II/5/22: He should be conversant with receipts from outside and inside even after a hundred years, so that when asked he would not falter in respect of expenditure, balance and collections.

The following *ślokas* contain prescriptions for inspection of the works of the officers of different government departments:

II/9/19: Therefore, he who is appointed by an order to a particular department shall communicate to him (i.e., the king) the real nature of that work and the income and expenditure (both) in detail and in the aggregate.

II/9/28: Therefore, his superintendents should carry out the works accompanied by accountants, writers, examiners of coins, receivers of balance and supervisors.

Accounting activities of the City-superintendent are described in the following *ślokas*:

II/36/1: The City Superintendent should look after the city in the manner of the Administrator.

II/36/2: The section officer (should look after) a group of ten families or twenty families or forty families.

II/36/3: He should find out the number of individuals, men and women, in that (group), according to caste, family-name and occupation, also their income and expenditure.

[For further details see **Book II, Chapters 6**, **19** and **35**].

Kauṭilya, like Manu, also mentions some benevolent activities of the state.

To quote:

I/19/34: In the happiness of the subjects lies the happiness of the king and in what is beneficial to the subjects, his own benefit. What is dear to himself is not beneficial to the king, but what is dear to the subjects is beneficial (to him).

This explains the basic attitude of the ruler towards his subjects – his basic purpose is not to gratify his personal welfare but the welfare of the subjects.

In distress and calamities afflicting the people, it is duty of the king to rescue them to the best of his capacity, and he should also take prior preparation for all exigencies.

II/1/36: The king should exempt from taxes a region laid waste by the army of an enemy or by foresters, or afflicted by disease or famine, and he should prohibit expensive sports.

II/15/22: From these he should set apart one-half for times of distress for the country people, (and) use the (other) half.

II/28/8: He should rescue boats that have gone out of their course or are tossed about by a gale, like a father.

II/28/9: He should make goods that have fallen in water either duty-free or pay half the duty.

For the role of the king in rescuing subjects from famine see *œloka* **IV/3/17** in **Chapter 3** of this study.

Provisions for the weaker sections are mentioned in the following *śloka*:

II/1/26: And, the king should maintain children, aged persons and persons in distress when they are helpless, as also the woman who has borne no child and the sons of one who has (when they are helpless).

Relevance for Modern India

In India after independence the rapid expansion of the state sector started mainly since the Second Five-Year Plan, which was based on the Mahalanobis model (a variant of the Feldman-Stalin model) of industrial development. Since then till the mid 1980s, there was continuous growth of the state sector and it encompassed almost all kinds of economic activities. The reasons put forward by the proponents of such an all-comprehensive state sector are mainly the following:

(i) Building up of infrastructure facilities, like transport and communications, irrigation, power etc.: The private sector entrepreneurs in India could not undertake these activities.

(ii) Establishing basic and capital goods industries like iron and steel, engineering, heavy chemicals, fertilizers, etc.: At the early stage of industrial development in India the private sector was reluctant to establish these industries, which required heavy initial investment but had a low rate of profit at the early stage. But establishment of these industries was necessary for laying the foundation of future industrial development of the country.

(iii) Employment generation: Profit motivated private sector was likely to disregard this aspect. So expansion of the state sector was necessary to reduce the intensity of the problem of unemployment.

(iv) Expansion of the social sector and provision of basic amenities like education, healthcare facilities, mass consumption goods, public goods etc.: This sector can by no means be left at the hands of the private sector and free play of market forces.

(v) Orderly management of the financial sector (banking, insurance etc.).

(vi) Regulation of foreign trade to reduce the balance of payments deficits.

Many of these arguments have, however, turned out to be very weak while others have validity only for a short period. For this reason, since the 1990s, privatization of the public sector enterprises has been undertaken. Even if, for arguments sake, we assume that vast state sector business activities are still necessary in India, the strongest objection would come from the standpoint of efficiency. In fact, the major reason for which the state sector in India failed to accomplish the tasks assigned to it is the overwhelming inefficiency and mismanagement of the state sector enterprises (Dhingra, 2000: 514-42).

Our discussion of the all-comprehensive role of the state sector in Arthaúâstra shows that it may be the policy for a specific historical situation but cannot be a permanent policy. Once the exigencies of the situation are over, the over-functioning state machinery is likely to become unnecessary and collapse under its own weight. This happened in recent decades in case of the major socialist states. Historically too, the Mauryan Empire collapsed after Emperor Aśoka. Many historians like Romila Thapar opined that the collapse was due mainly to the too much expansion of the functions of the state leading to heavy financial requirements (to run the state machinery) that could not be afforded through the mechanisms of revenue collection (Thapar, 1961). The all-powerful state machinery as prescribed in the Arthaśāstra had emerged as a historical necessity and it collapsed as soon as the historical necessity was no longer in existence.

After achievement of independence, the Indian economy was in shambles. So, it was necessary to revive the economy and initiate the process of economic development through planning and rapid expansion of the state sector. But, as the Indian economy is no longer in a situation where state initiative in all sectors is necessary, the era of comprehensive planning, vast state sector and widespread regulations has come to an end. That is why, the policy of liberalization and privatization has been undertaken since 1991. So, the question arises whether we can learn from Arthaśāstra of Kauṭilya, which prescribed for all-comprehensive activities of the state.

Although all-embracing state sector economic activities are no longer desirable in India today, there are many areas where proper development is not possible without direct participation of the state. The most important areas calling for direct government participation are public goods and merit goods like infrastructural facilities (roads, bridges, irrigation works, street lighting etc.), healthcare facilities for common people, mass education etc. These sectors have high external economies so that private output is always far below the socially desirable one. For example, let us consider the case of mass education. At present universal education is an urgent necessity in India. But the majority of the population are not capable of paying for education because of poverty. The private sector can provide educational facilities to the well-to-do minority who are able to make adequate payments that cover the cost plus minimum required profit of the private operators. For provision of mass education, direct participation of the state is essential. If necessary, the cooperation of philanthropic NGOs may be sought in this regard.

However, in many cases, provision of public utilities leads to the problem of 'free-riders'. For example, if a private company wants to provide street-lighting, it will have to collect the expenses from the residents by the side of the street. But the intelligent residents will decline to pay on the plea that they do not require street-lighting. They know that if others provide the expenses and the lighting facilities are installed, nobody can prevent them from walking along the lighted street at night.

In recent years all the countries have been emphasising on the changing role of the state, which is more concerned about the development of the social sector. It has been realized that *laissez-faire* is not necessary for perfect operation of the market mechanism and social sector development by the state may go hand in hand with the free-market economy. This is an important area where the state has to directly intervene.

In this manner we can identify many areas where direct state participation is not only justified but is also essential even in the era of liberalization. But these sectors are to be identified properly and operated efficiently with least possible corruption. The basic problems of the state sector in India today are inefficiency and widespread corruption. Here, we may take lessons from Kauṭilya's Arthaśāstra, which specifies in detail how state sector activities could be run efficiently and with least possible corruption. Its coherent prescriptions for discipline and accounting, punishment for violation of rules and negligence of assigned duties, punitive measures for corrupt officials etc. are likely to be of considerable help to make the state initiative, in the selected areas, run efficiently and with least possible corruption. This is the lesson from and relevance of the Arthaśāstra for India today.

References

Dhingra, I.C. (2000): *The Indian Economy: Environment and Policy*, Sultan Chand & Sons, New Delhi.

Thapar, R. (1961): *Asoka and the Decline of the Mauryas*, Oxford University Press.

7

Price Policy

Price Control for Selected Commodities

Price policy was an integral part of state policy in ancient India. It appears from ancient Indian texts that due regard was paid to demand and supply in price determination. Prices were to be ultimately determined on the basis of cost of production on the one hand and intensity of demand on the other but the just price, was to be ensured by the state. The state could not fix prices arbitrarily disregarding market forces, but had to see to it that traders and producers could not manipulate prices to make exorbitant profit, could not cheat the buyers or create crisis by taking advantage of shortages. Ancient authors, particularly Kautilya, were well aware of the psychology of the businessmen who, if left alone would distort free play of the market mechanism and charge exorbitant prices, out of greed. So, either the state should determine the prices, or prices announced by the traders and producers should be approved by the state – both on the basis of the concept of 'just price' and the forces of demand and supply.

In case of temporary discrepancy (excess demand or excess supply), prices were not permitted to increase or fall, but were fixed at a given level till the discrepancy passed off. In case the discrepancy persisted, the state never attempted to keep prices rigid. In this situation, prices were increased (in case of excess demand) or reduced (in case of excess supply) step by step and by the process of 'trial-and-error' so as to arrive at a new equilibrium restoring balance between demand and supply. But, in this regard, private persons were never given a free hand. Prices were readjusted either directly by the state, or the revised prices were announced by the sellers on the basis of approval by the state. Now, we examine the specific measures in this regard in Manusmṛti and Arthaśāstra of Kauṭilya.

Manusmṛti

In Manusmṛti it is opined that the state, by considering cost of production, other expenses, demand, supply etc., should fix the price of each commodity every five days or every fortnight, as is evident from the following *ślokas*:

8/401: Let (the king) fix (the rates for) the purchase and sale of all marketable goods, having (duly) considered whence they come, whither they go, how long they have been kept, the (probable) profit and the (probable) outlay.

8/402: Once in five nights, or at the close of each fortnight, let the king publicly settle the prices for the (merchants).

Manu opines in this regard that weighing balance and weighing stones should be checked and approved by the government officials every six months.

8/403: All weights and measures must be duly marked, and once in six months let him re-examine them.

Rules for Wages

Wages and fees are to be determined by contract between the employer and the employee, and once made the contract should be legally binding on both the parties.

To quote:

7/125: For the women engaged in royal services and for the menials, he should fix (and pay them) daily wages according to position and work.

7/126: To an inferior (i.e., menial) servant one *paṇa* should be given as the wages (per diem) and a pair of clothes every six months and a *droṇa* of paddy every month. To a superior servant six *paṇas* are to be given. (N.B. other conditions too, are to be altered accordingly).

8/231: A hired herdsman who is paid with milk, may milk with the consent of the owner the best (cow) out of ten; such shall be his hire if no (other) wages (are paid).

8/232: The herdsman alone shall make good (the loss of a beast) strayed, destroyed by worms, killed by dogs or (by falling) into a pit, if he did not duly exert himself (to prevent it).

8/396: A washerman shall wash (the clothes of his employers) gently on a smooth board of *Śālmalī* wood; he shall not return the clothes (of one person) for those (of another), nor allow anybody (but the owner) to wear them.

8/397: A weaver (who has received) ten *palas* (of thread), shall return (cloth weighing) one *pala* more; he who acts differently shall be compelled to pay a fine of twelve (*paṇas*).

In the following *ślokas*, Manu prescribes how the fees for a work performed jointly are to be shared among the participants:

8/208: But if (specific) fees are ordained for the several parts of a rite, shall he (who performs the part) receive them, or shall they all share them?

8/209: The *Adhvaryu* priest shall take the chariot, and the *Brāhmaṇa* at the kindling of the fires (*Agnyādhāna*) a horse, the *Hotṛ* priest shall also take a horse, and the *Udgātṛ* the cart, (used) when (the *Soma*) is purchased.

8/210: The (four) chief priests among all (the sixteen), who are entitled to one half, shall receive a moiety (of the fee), the next (four) one half of that, the set entitled to a third share, one-third, and those entitled to a fourth a quarter.

8/211: By the application of these principles the allotment of shares must be made among those men who here (below) perform their work conjointly.

Laws for those who break a work agreement: Manu prescribes various punishments including non-payment of wages for breaking contracts:

8/215: A hired (servant or workman) who, without being ill, out of pride fails to perform his work according to the agreement, shall be fined eight *Kṛṣṇalas* and no wages shall be paid to him.

8/216: But (if he is really) ill, (and) after recovery performs (his work) according to the original agreement, he shall receive his wages even after (the lapse of) a very long time.

8/217: But if he, whether sick or well, does not (perform or) cause to be performed (by others) his work according to his agreement, the wages for that work shall not be given to him, even (if it be only) slightly incomplete.

8/218: Thus the law for the non-payment of wages has been completely stated; I will next explain the law concerning men who break an agreement.

8/156: He who has made a contract to carry goods by a wheeled carriage for money and has agreed to a certain place or time, shall not reap that reward, if he does not keep to the place and the time (stipulated).

8/206: If an officiating priest, chosen to perform a sacrifice, abandons his work, a share only (of the fee) in proportion to the work (done) shall be given to him by those who work with him.

8/207: But he who abandons his work after the sacrificial fees have been given, shall obtain his full share and cause to be performed (what remains) by another (priest).

8/219: If a man belonging to a corporation inhabiting a village or a district, after swearing to an agreement, breaks it through avarice, (the king) shall banish him from his realm.

8/220: And having imprisoned such a breaker of an agreement, he shall compel him to pay six *niṣkas*, (each of) four *Suvarṇas*, and one *Satamāna* of silver.

8/221: A righteous king shall apply this law of fines in villages and castes (*jāti*) to those who break an agreement.

Interest

Manu suggests an annual interest rate of 24 per cent for the Brāhmaṇa, 36 per cent for the *Kṣatriya*, 48 per cent for the *Vaiśya*, and 60 per cent for the *Śūdra*.

8/141: Or, remembering the duty of good men, he may take two in the hundred (by the month), for he who takes two in the hundred becomes not a sinner for gain.

8/142: Just two in the hundred, three, four, and five (and not more), he may take as monthly interest according to the order of the castes (*varṇa*).

It appears from the above *ślokas* that interest rate increases according to inferiority of caste. This may be justified on the ground that at Manu's time, caste was determined by the qualities of a person – *Brāhmaṇa* possessing the highest *sātvika* qualities and *Sudras,* the lowest *tāmasika* qualities, the intensities of *sātvika* quality declining and *tāmasika* qualities increasing with increase in order of castes. Manu discouraged spending (by borrowing) by *Śūdras* who were mainly guided by *tāmasika* qualities and were likely to misuse the loan money. *Brāhmaṇa* on the other hand, being guided mainly by *sātvika* attributes were likely to spend most judiciously. So, interest rate was highest for the *Śūdras* and lowest for the *Brāhmaṇa*.

Other Rules for Interest

8/143: But if a beneficial pledge (i.e., one from which profit accrues, has been given), he shall receive no interest on the loan; nor can he, after keeping (such) a pledge for a very long time, give or sell it.

8/144: A pledge (to be kept only) must not be used by force, (the creditor), so using it, shall give up his (whole) interest, or, (if it has been spoilt by use) he shall satisfy the (owner) by (paying its) original price; else he commits a theft of the pledge.

8/151: In money transactions interest paid at one time (not by instalments) shall never exceed the double (of the principal); on grain, fruit, wool or hair, (and) beasts of burden it must not be more than five times (the original amount).

8/152: Stipulated interest beyond the legal rate, being against (the law), cannot be recovered; they call that a usurious way (of lending); (the lender) is (in no case) entitled to (more than) five in the hundred.

8/153: Let him not take interest, beyond the year, not such as is unapproved, nor compound interest, periodic interest, stipulated interest and corporal interest.

8/154: He who, unable to pay a debt (at the fixed time), wishes to make a new contract, may renew the agreement, after paying the interest which is due.

8/155: If he cannot pay the money (due as interest), he may insert it in the renewed (agreement); he must pay as much interest as may be due.

8/157: Whatever rate men fix, who are expert in sea-voyages and able to calculate (the profit) according to the place, the time, and the objects (carried), that (has legal force) in such cases with respect to the payment (to be made).

8/158: The man who becomes a surety in this (world) for the appearance of a (debtor), and produces him not, shall pay the debt out of his own property.

8/159: But money due by a surety, or idly promised, or lost at play, or due for spirituous liquor, or what remains unpaid of a fine and a tax or duty, the son (of the party owing it) shall not be obliged to pay.

8/163: A contract made by a person intoxicated, or insane, or grievously disordered (by disease and so forth), or wholly dependent, by an infant or very aged man, or by an unauthorized (party) is invalid.

8/166: If the debtor be dead and (the money borrowed) was expended for the family, it must be paid by the relatives out of their own estate even if they are divided.

8/167: Should even a person wholly dependent make a contract for the behoof of the family, the master (of the house), whether (living) in his own country or abroad, shall not rescind it.

8/177: Even by (personal) labour shall the debtor make good (what he owes) to his creditor, if he be of the same caste or of a lower one; but a (debtor) of a higher caste shall pay it gradually (when he earns something).

Ferry Charges

8/404: At a ferry an (empty) cart shall be made to pay one *paṇa*, a man's (load) half a *paṇa*, an animal and a woman one quarter of a (*paṇa*), an unloaded man one-half of a quarter.

8/406: For a long passage the boat-hire must be proportioned to the places and times; know that this (rule refers) to (passages along) the banks of rivers; at sea there is no settled (freight).

Restrictions on the Traders

In the following *śloka*, Manu prescribes prohibition of adulteration, sales of low quality or underweight commodities and other means of cheating the buyer:

8/203: One commodity mixed with another must not be sold (as pure), nor a bad one (as good), nor less (than the proper quantity or weight), nor anything that is not at hand or that is concealed.

The following *śloka* mentions the legal opportunity of buyers and sellers to change their decision after the transaction has taken place.

8/222: If anybody in this (world) after buying or selling anything, repent (of his bargain), he may return or take (back) that chattel within ten days.

The following *śloka* mentions the rules of punishment of the violators of laws pertaining to export of commodities.

8/399: see Chapter 5 above.

Arthaśāstra

The actual measures to fix and alter prices and the measures to implement them have been delineated in more detail in Arthaśāstra of Kauṭilya. According to Arthaśāstra, the superintendent of commerce was entrusted with the task of enforcing the price policy. The prices of different commodities were to be fixed by him. He, however, did not fix prices arbitrarily. In fact, a uniform rule was followed throughout the country to determine the 'just price' of each commodity [see **Book IV, Chapter 2**].

Just price was defined as:

Just price = average cost of production + tolls and taxes

+ transport and associated costs + profit margin.

where,

Production cost = cost of raw materials + wages + interest.

Now, one may be tempted to compare this 'just price' with other similar concepts available in the jungle of modern economic literature. But, a little reflection will make one realize that such comparisons do not make sense. There are innumerable normative approaches and value judgments as regards determination of fair price or just price and each modern scholar unleashes his theoretical swords (without any real world connotation) to substantiate his own point. But, in Arthaśāstra, this concept of 'just price' was a real world phenomenon and sprang directly from the ancient Indian world outlook of balance embedded in the text. According to Arthaśāstra, prices are to be so determined as to strike a balance between the interests of the buyers and that of the sellers. To fulfill this objective, the following guidelines are recommended in Arthaśāstra.

Goods are to be sold at places specified by the state and prices should be announced (for approval by the state and knowledge of the buyers) by the businessmen.

II/22/9: And no sale of commodities (shall be allowed) in the places of their origin.

II/21/7: Traders shall declare the quantity and price of the goods that have arrived at the foot of the flag, 'Who is willing to purchase these goods, so much in quantity, at this price?'

Goods should bear official 'seal' and should be properly weighed, measured and numbered. Violation of this rule was subject to punishment.

To quote:

II/21/3: For (goods) without the stamp the penalty is double the dues.

II/21/4: For those with a forged stamp, the fine is eight times the duty.

II/21/5: For those with broken stamps, the penalty is distraint in the ware-house.

II/21/6: In case of change of the royal stamp or of (change in) the name, he should make (the trader) pay a fine of one *paṇa* and a quarter per load.

II/21/15: Therefore, the sale of goods should be made by weighing, measuring or counting; an appraisal (of value should be made) of goods of small value and goods enjoying concessions.

The following *ślokas* describe the punishments for false declaration by the traders.

II/21/10: If for fear of duty a (trader) declares the quantity of the goods or the price to be less (than it actually is), the king shall confiscate that excess.

II/21/11: Or, the (trader) shall pay eight times the duty.

II/21/12: He should impose the same (penalty) in case of depreciation of price of a package containing goods by (showing) a sample of lower value and in case of concealment of goods of high value by goods of low value.

Enhancement of price by bidding was discouraged.

II/21/13: Or, if through fear of a rival purchaser a (trader) increases the price beyond the (due) price of a commodity, the king shall receive the increase in price, or make the amount of duty double.

The following *śloka* prescribes how the government officials, who took underhand means to guard the guilty merchants (accepting bribe etc.), are to be punished:

II/21/14: The same (penalty) eightfold (shall be imposed) on the Superintendent concealing (the trader's offences).

Kauṭilya also provides detailed guidelines for determination of various components of price.

Wages

Guidelines for wage determination are scattered in **Book III, Chapters 13, 14**; **Book IV, Chapter 2** and **Book V, Chapter 3** of Arthaśāstra. The basic principles of wage-determination, as prescribed in these chapters, were that wages should be so determined (by contract between the employer and the employee, which once settled, would be binding on both the parties) that the employer is not cheated and at the same time the employee is not exploited. Violation of contract by either party would be subjected to punishment. Wages are to be determined on the basis of existing customs where they are available.

To quote:

III/13/26: Those who are near shall note a labourer's engagement in work.

III/13/27: He should receive a wage as agreed upon, in conformity with the work and time (if the wage is not agreed upon).

For cases where wages are not negotiated or determined by some existing local custom, Kauṭilya prescribes some rules for determination of wages.

To quote:

III/13/28: A cultivator, a cowherd (and) a trader should receive one-tenth part of the crops, of butter (and) of the goods dealt in by them (respectively) if the wage is not agreed upon.

III/13/29: But if the wage is agreed upon, then as agreed upon.

III/13/30: But the group of those who work in hope (of remuneration) such as artisans, artists, minstrels, physicians, professional story-tellers, attendants and others should get a remuneration, as others of that type do or as experts fix.

The prescriptions for settlements of disputes regarding work are to be found in the following *ślokas*:

III/13/31: (Disputes) shall be settled only on the testimony of witnesses.

III/13/32: In the absence of witnesses, (the judge) should inquire at the place where the work (was carried out).

Non-payment of wages by the employers is punishable.

To quote:

III/13/33: In case of non-payment of the wage, the fine is one-tenth or six *paṇas*.

III/13/34: In case of denial, the fine is twelve *paṇas* or one-fifth.

Wages in the state sector were determined in various ways. One important aspect of state sector employment of labourers is the provision of incentives through gifts etc. to the efficient labourers.

To quote:

II/23/3: He should fix the wage after ascertaining the fineness, coarseness or medium quality of the yarn, and the largeness or smallness of quantity.

II/23/4: After finding out the amount of yarn, he should favour them with oil and myrobalan unguents.

II/23/5: And on festive days, they should be made to work by honouring (them) and making gifts.

II/23/6: In case of diminution in yarn, (there shall be) a diminution in wage, according to the value of the stuff.

II/23/7: And he should cause work to be carried out by artisans producing goods with an agreement as to the amount of work, time and wage, and should maintain close contact with them.

[For ***ślokas*** **II/23/1** and **II/23/2** see **Chapter 4** of this study].

There is also a long list of wages of various state-sector employees as described in **Book V, Chapter 3** of Arthaśāstra. Some of them are given below:

Salaries of Government Employees

48,000 *Paṇas* **[V/3/3]:** (i) Sacrificial Priest, (ii) Preceptor, (iii) Chaplain, (iv) Minister, (v) Commander-in Chief, (vi) Crown Prince, (vii) King's Mother, (viii) Crowned Queen.

V/3/4: With this much remuneration, they become insusceptible to instigations and disinclined to revolt.

24,000 *Paṇas* **[V/3/5]:** (i) Chief Palace Usher, (ii) Chief Palace Guards, (iii) Director (of labour corps), (iv) Administrator, (v) Director of Stores.

V/3/6: With this much, they become efficient in their work.

12,000 *Paṇas* **[V/3/7]:** (i) Princes, (ii) Mothers of Princes, (iii) Commandant, (iv) City Judge, (v) Director of Factories, (vi) Provincial Officer, (vii) Council of Ministers, (viii) Frontier Officer.

V/3/8: For, with this much, they help in strengthening the entourage of the master.

8,000 *Paṇas* **[V/3/9]:** (i) Heads of Banded Troops, (ii) Commandant of Elephants, Horses and Chariot Corps, (iii) Magistrates.

V/91/3/10: For, with this much, they are able to carry their groups with them.

4,000 *Paṇas* [**V/3/11]:** (i) Superintendents of Infantry, Cavalry, Chariots and Elephants, (ii) Guardians of materials and Elephant-forests.

2,000 *Paṇas* **[V/3/12]:** (i) Chariot-fighter, (ii) Elephant-trainer, (ii) Physician, (iii) Horse-trainer, (iv) Carpenter, (v) Breeders of Animals.

1,000 *Paṇas* **[V/3/13]:** (i) Fortune-teller, (ii) Soothsayer, (iii) Astrologer, (iv) Narrator of Purāṇas, (v) King's Charioteer **[V/3/21]**, (vi) Bard, (vii) Chaplain's Men, (viii) All Superintendents, (ix) Sharp Pupils, Monks Fallen from Vow, and Agents Appearing as House-holders, Traders and Ascetics **[V/3/22]**.

500-1000 *Paṇas,* according to merit **[V/3/13]:** (i) Teachers and Learned Men, (ii) Elephant Driver, (iii) Sorcerer, (iv) Miners of Mountains, (v) All kinds of Attendants, Teachers & Learned Men, (vi) Spies.

500 *Paṇas* **[V/3/14:** (i) Foot-soldiers trained in the (fighting) arts, (ii) Groups of accountants, clerks and others, (iii) Makers of Musical Instruments **[V/3/15]**, (iv) Village Servants, Secret Agents, Assassins, Poison-givers and Female Mendicants **[V/3/23]**.

250 *Paṇas* **[V/3/15]:** (i) Actors, (ii) those moving about for Spying **[V/3/24]**.

120 *Paṇas* **[V/3/16]:** (i) Artisans, (ii) Artists.

60 *Paṇas* **[V/3/17]:** (i) Servants, valets, attendants and guards of Quadrupeds and Bipeds, (ii) Foremen of Labourers, (iii) All Attendants, (iv) Riders, Bandits and Mountain-diggers supervised by Āryas.

10 *Paṇas/yojana* up to 10 *yojanas* and 20 *Paṇas/yojana* beyond 10 *yojanas* **[V/3/19]:** (i) The Average Envoy.

[For other detailed information about the principle of wage determination in specific case, see **Book III, Chapter 14** and **Book IV, Chapter 1** of Arthaśāstra].

Interest

Interest rates are to be rigidly fixed by the state (considering the degree of risk involved) so as to prevent usury and exploitation of the weak borrowers.

III/11/1: One *paṇa* and a quarter is the lawful rate of interest per month on one hundred *paṇas*, five *paṇas* for purposes of trade, ten *paṇas* for those going through forests, twenty *paṇas* for those going by sea.

III/11/2: For one charging or making another charge a rate beyond that, the punishment shall be the lowest fine for violence, for witnesses, each one of them, half the fine.

III/11/3: If, however, the king is unable to ensure protection, the (judge) should take into consideration the usual practice among creditors and debtors.

III/11/4: Interest on grains (shall be) up to a half, on the harvesting crops; thereafter it may increase being turned into capital.

III/11/5: Interest on capital (shall amount to) half the profit, to be paid for one year, being set apart in a store.

From the above excerpt it turns out that annual interest:

For non-commercial loans = 15 per cent

For less risky commercial loans = 60 per cent

For risky commercial loans = 120 per cent and

For foreign trade = 240 per cent.

If we look closely at the above chart, we shall find that the rate of interest on loans for foreign trade (24% per annum) was much higher than that on loans for internal trade. This is quite contrary to the present day state policy pursued in India where, considering the chronic balance of payments crisis, it is desirable that interest on loans for foreign trade, especially for exports, should be lower than that on loans for internal trade. One probable explanation of higher rate of interest on loans for foreign trade could be that invasion by Alexander the Great generated a feeling of xeno-phobia in India at that time. It was apprehended that foreign trade would reveal to the foreigners the vast resources of our country and would, thereby, lure them to invade India. So to avoid foreign invasion, foreign trade was discouraged.

But this is a very weak argument. A more feasible explanation lies in the risk factor in different kind of loans. In those days transport and communication systems were undeveloped; so foreign trade was much more hazardous than internal trade. Also, modern commercial banks and lending institutions were non-existent in those days and most of the private money-lenders were not much resourceful. So, the risk factor used to play a dominant role in determining the rate of interest.

A close look at the chart for interest rates above shows that even in case of internal trade, interest rate increases according to the degree of hazards involved in trading. Interest rate on loans for hazardous internal trade (120% per annum) is double of that on loans for hazard-free internal trade (60% per annum). By the same logic one may conclude that interest rate on loans for foreign trade, which involved much more hazards (than internal trade), would be higher in general as compared to interest rates on loans for internal trade.

Profit

Profit rates should also be rigidly fixed by the state so as to avoid uncertainty and to prevent traders from profiteering. There are also specific guidelines for ascertaining transport, storage and other associated expenses. Rigid and simplified rules must be observed for determining tolls and taxes on all the commodities produced and traded. The following extract is relevant in this regard.

IV/2/28: And he should fix a profit for them of five per hundred over and above the permitted purchase-price in the case of indigenous commodities, ten (per hundred) in the case of foreign goods.

Any trader, trying to earn a higher profit than prescribed by the state, will be punished.

To quote:

IV/2/29: For those who increase the price beyond that or secure (a profit beyond that) during purchase or sale, the fine shall be two hundred *paṇas* for (an additional profit of) five *paṇas* in one hundred *paṇas*.

Rules for Determining Prices of Goods Sold through Selling Agents

III/12/25: Concerning sale through agents, however, salesmen selling the commodity at the proper place and time shall pay (to the owner) the price as received and the profit.

III/12/26: Or, if (the price is) lower because of their missing the proper place and time, they shall pay the price according to the rate at the time of giving (the goods to them for sale) and the profit.

III/23/27: Or, if selling (the goods) as agreed upon they do not make a profit, they should pay only the price.

II/23/28: Or, if the price is lower because of a fall in prices, they should give the lower price as reduced.

II/23/29: Or, in the case of dealers, who are trustworthy and free from blame so far as the king is concerned, they may not pay even the price of what is lost or ruined through deterioration or a sudden calamity.

II/23/30: But of commodities removed in space or time they shall pay the price and profit after deducting losses and expenses, and a separate share in the case of each of the different kinds of goods.

Unnecessary controls were always avoided in the Arthaśāstra price policy. The officer in charge of commodities was entrusted with the task of fixing or altering prices, depending on the objective conditions. He also determined the rules for sales of royal commodities and commodities imported from abroad.

[Also see **Book II, Chapter 16** of Arthaśāstra**].**

Implementation

Price policy in Arthaśāstra was inexorably associated with the methods of implementation, which consisted of: (a) administrative measures; (b) accounting; and (c) buffer stock.

Administrative Measures

As regards implementation of price policy, a crucial role was played by the superintendent of the toll house. Simultaneously with collection of tolls, he was entrusted with the task of implementing prices fixed by the superintendent of commerce. If the concerned officials shirked their duties or adopted corrupt practices in connivance with the traders, they were punished [see **II/21/14** above].

The espionage network used to play an important role in the implementation of price policy. False statements regarding costs and prices, adulteration, smuggling, overvaluation, undervaluation, etc. by the merchants, could not have been prevented without the help of the spies.

Government officials, entrusted with the task of implementing price policy, could not resort to corrupt practices as spies in different guises were looming at every corner. Anybody, whatever his apparent identity, might have been a disguised spy and so the fear of being detected and punished discouraged merchants and government officials from resorting to underhand practices or violating rules and procedures of price control laid down by the state.

To quote:

II/21/17: Secret agents operating on roads and in places without roads should find out such (evasion).

II/21/27: Or, a secret agent appearing as a trader should communicate to the king the size of the caravan.

[Also see **Book II, Chapter 35** of Arthaśāstra].

"There were spies in every traders' caravan" (Kosambi 1981: 147).

The espionage network facilitated perfect implementation of price policy by ensuring: (i) dissemination of correct information relevant to costs and prices, and (ii) prevention of corruption.

Accounting

We have discussed in detail the role of perfect auditing and accounting, in **Chapter 5** of this study.

Buffer Stock

In Arthaśāstra much emphasis is laid on the maintenance of a buffer stock of all commodities so as to meet accidental shortages and thereby, to ensure smooth implementation of the price policy [For details see **Book II**, **Chapters 5** and **15** of Arthaśāstra].

Relevance for Modern India

The price policy in ancient texts, especially in Arthaśāstra, was basically designed for monarchy. So, the question arises whether it has any relevance for the democratic India today. If we closely study the price policy in Arthaśāstra and the suggested measures to implement them, it would be clear that none of them is contradictory to the provisions of the Constitution of democratic India today. In fact, the policy sprang from the basic Indian world outlook of balance and harmony. Price control is necessary to ensure this harmony because activities associated with profit and accumulation of wealth inherently contains the unbalancing factor of 'greed'. So, unless restrained by the state, pricing by traders and producers would automatically generate disharmony. So, whatever be the form of the government, according to the ancient Indian world outlook, it must run, in conformity with dharma and should impose dharma on all material activities (pursuits of *artha* and *kāma*) to assure harmony and balance. This is a basic outlook and not conditioned by the form of the government.

As regards the necessity of price control in India today, L.K.Jha, the ex-Governor of the Reserve Bank of India, pointed out that prices in an LDC like India cannot be left to be determined by market forces where, instead of free competition, monopolistic control prevails. According to Jha, direct price-control becomes necessary in India for the following reasons:

(i) To protect the interests of the vulnerable sections of the population;
(ii) To guide investment to the desired channels; and
(iii) To prevent hoarders from increasing prices by taking advantage of shortages (Jha, 1968: 478-80).

Thus, we se that in spite of the differences in the political systems, the basic objective of ancient Indian price policy resembles the 'administered price policy' under the Five-Year

Plans in India. But, the ancient Indian price policy distinguishes itself for the following reasons:

(i) Unlike in India today, monetary and fiscal policies were not used for price control in ancient India. Only direct price-control measures were applied.

(ii) Unnecessary controls were always avoided in ancient India.

(iii) Prices were rigidly fixed by the state only when discrepancies between demand and supply were temporary. In case of persistent discrepancies, prices were permitted to vary according to market forces of demand and supply. But even in such a case, suitable adjustments were made by the state or, revised prices proposed by the sellers were to be approved by the state. Private sellers were never permitted to do such revisions on their own.

(iv) Price policy was accompanied by suitable administrative and legal measures for its proper implementation.

The basic features of price policy pursued in India during the plan period were:

(i) Administered prices for various agricultural and industrial commodities;

(ii) Vast subsidies arising out of the endeavour to fulfil simultaneously the contradictory objectives of providing price incentives to the producers and provision of low-priced essential goods to the consumers.

The above features, however, have led to many undesirable effects on the Indian economy. The Seventh and Eighth Plan documents (Planning Commission), various issues of the Report on Currency and Finance (RBI), and Economic Survey (Government of India) have revealed many disquieting features of the administered price policy in India. In fact, instead of having control over the prices, the price-controlling authorities are themselves being controlled by extraneous forces, which compel them to raise prices in inappropriate moments leading to many adverse repercussions on the economy.

So, to avoid the adverse impacts of a badly conceived and badly managed price policy and to devise a proper price policy, the government of India at present can take the following lessons from the ancient texts, particularly, Arthaśāstra of Kauṭilya.

(i) The market mechanism should not be interfered with unnecessarily. The government should interfere only when it is necessary, e.g., when monopolies or vested-interest groups try to obstruct the smooth functioning of the market mechanism, when traders and hoarders try to complicate the situation of shortage and fish out of troubled water, etc.

(ii) There should be appropriate administrative and legal set up for proper implementation of the price policy, as in Arthaśāstra. We may tone up our administrative and legal systems and emulate many features of Arthaśāstra economy in this regard, without violating any provisions of our democratic political set up.

One strong objection against Kauṭilya's measures is related to the exhaustive espionage network of Kauṭilya. This may be contrary to ideal democratic norms. But, in a limited scale, an efficient intelligence network is necessary under all systems to maintain administrative efficiency and to suppress corruption. Secret agencies like the CBI (Central Bureau of Investigations), Intelligence Branch, Special Branch, Enforcement Branch, Vigilance Departments etc., are essential for proper functioning of the government, and to fight against crime and corruption. Nobody is likely to consider the CBI's actions against the unscrupulous politicians undemocratic.

Moreover, the vast espionage network of Kauṭilya was an alternative to the quick transport and communication facilities, which were lacking in those days (Mukherjee, 1976: 42).

Nowadays, these tasks of Kauṭilya's spies could be easily handled by computers and the Internet.

So, it is likely that emulation of these basic features of ancient Indian price policy would convert our ill-administered price policy under planning into a well-administered one, which would be capable of restoring balance in the market mechanism, facilitating unhindered functioning of the market mechanism, and bringing about welfare of the majority of the population of the country.

It is desirable that prices of most of the commodities are determined by the forces of the market. But prices of some sensitive commodities should be fixed and directly regulated by the state. At present the list of commodities for administered pricing are haphazardly selected, and at times, at the behest of the vested interest groups. This is not at all desirable. The question is one of selecting the appropriate commodities for which prices are to be administered by the state.

References

Government of India: *Economic Survey*, Various Issues

Government of India, Planning Commission: *7th, 8th and 9th Plan Documents.*

Jha, L.K. (1968): "Price Policy in a Developing Economy", *Reserve Bank of India Bulletin*, April.

Kosambi, D.D. (1981): *The Culture and Civilization of Ancient India*, Vikas Publishing House, New Delhi.

Mukherjee, B. (1976): *Kautilya's Concept of Diplomacy*, Minerva Associates Pvt. Ltd., Calcutta.

Reserve Bank of India: *Report on Currency and Finance*, Various Issues.

8

Taxation and Fiscal Policy

Direct versus Indirect Taxes and Fiscal Management

Tax has been the major source of revenue of the government from the very ancient times. Even today, it is the most important source of revenue of modern governments. The advantage of taxes is that the money collected from this source is not to be returned to the payer, payment of taxes (by those on whom taxes are imposed) is compulsory, and no direct benefits are to be provided to the payers in exchange for tax payments. Moreover, tax policy may be used as an important fiscal instrument for regulating the economy. Nowadays, tax system has become extremely complicated because of increasing complexity of the economic system. So, the question arises whether the ancient tax policies have any relevance for modern India. To examine this, let us first discuss the tax policies as delineated in Manusmṛti and Arthaśāstra of Kauṭilya.

Manusmṛti

The basic principles of tax policy in ancient India are clearly defined in Manusmṛti. They are: Taxes should be so imposed that they do not result in disincentive for production and trading activities. At the same time, tax collection should be adequate to cover the expenses of the state.

To quote:

7/128: The king should fix taxes in his kingdom after such consideration that he himself and the workers (traders, cultivators, etc.) achieve adequate results.

The proper method to realize such an end is clearly defined in the following *ślokas*.

7/129: As the leech, the calf and the bee take their food little by little, so should the king draw from his realm revenue on a small scale.

7/137: The king should make the ordinary men living on (small) trades in his kingdom, pay something, however small, annually in the shape of tax.

7/138: He should have his work done for one day every month by artisans, mechanics and *Śūdras* who subsist by bodily labour.

This implies that everybody in the state should be taxed mildly. Even the poor should pay some tax, whatever little the amount. This has many implications. First, too much burden should not fall on a few persons (which generates unpopularity of the tax and encourages tax evasion, resulting in revenue loss of the state and disincentives to save and invest). Secondly, tax payment generates involvement of the payee in state activities resulting in civic and political consciousness among all citizens.

Tax should be collected with adherence to the Vedic principles and officials are to be appointed for tax collection. This basic outline of the procedure of tax collection is stated in the following *śloka*:

7/80: See Chapter 5 above.

How to employ honest officials and methods of vigilance over the employees are explained in the following *ślokas*.

7/81: He should appoint expert supervisors in every department and they should supervise the works of his officers.

7/122: He (the superintendent) should (if required) personally (with his forces) attend all these (chiefs), (and the king) should acquaint himself with the conduct of all these officers in the kingdom through spies in particular places.

All villagers are to contribute whatever they can, for the state. These, while collected together, may contribute considerably towards meeting expenses for the local bodies, as stated in the following *śloka*:

7/118: The articles of food, drink and fuel, which are to be given unto the king daily by the villagers, the chief of the village should obtain (for his livelihood).

The other relevant matters like rules of tax collection, tax rates on different commodities etc. are described below:

Basic Rules of Tax Fixation

Taxes should be imposed so as to get the best possible result and they should not cause disincentive. While imposing taxes on the commodities traded by the merchants consideration should be given not only to the total cost of the articles but also to the daily essential living expenses of the merchants.

To quote:

7/127: After having considered the cost of purchase, the sale price, the cost of conveyance, the cost of food together with necessaries, the cost of insurance and the net profit, he should make the merchants pay taxes.

Taxes should be so imposed as to achieve best possible results in terms of revenue of the state as well as work efficiency. That is a perfect balance is to be maintained between revenue collection of the government and the work incentives of the payees see *śloka* 7/128 above.

To quote:

7/128: See above.

There should not be too little taxation as this will lead to inadequacy of revenue. On the other hand, too much taxation should also be avoided because that would generate disincentive and inclination to evade tax payment.

To quote:

7/139: He should not destroy his own root (by total remission of rent) nor that of others (i.e., the subjects) by an inordinate thirst. By destroying his own roots he afflicts himself, and (by destroying the root of others) he afflicts others.

All aspects pertaining to the taxable commodities are to be considered before finalizing the tax rates.

To quote:

8/401: Let (the king) fix (the rates for) the purchase and sale of all marketable goods, having (duly) considered whence they come, whither they go, how long they have been kept, the (probable) profit and the (probable) outlay.

Tax Rates on Various Commodities

7/130: Of cattle and gold (as profit) the king should get one-fiftieth part. Of crops, he should have the sixth, the eighth or the twelfth.

7/131: But he should have one-sixth of (the profit derived from) trees, meat, honey, clarified butter, perfumes (medicinal), herbs, flavouring articles, flower, roots, fruits.

7/132: Leaves, vegetables, grass, things made of bamboo, skin, earthen articles and all articles made of stone.

8/404: See Chapter 6 above.

8/405: Carts (laden) with vessels full (of merchandise) shall be made to pay toll at a ferry according to the value (of the goods), empty vessels and men without luggage some trifle.

Penalties for Violation of Rules

8/399: See Chapter 5 above.

8/400: He who avoids a custom house (or a toll), he who buys or sells at an improper time, or he who makes a false statement in enumerating (his goods), shall be fined eight times (the amount of duty) which he tried to evade.

Exemptions

8/407: See Chapter 5 above.

From the above discussion it appears that most of the taxes prescribed by Manu were indirect taxes; the basic principle was that tax rates should not be too high or too low, they should not exert much pressure on anybody generating disincentive; taxes should be collected from everybody, whatever small be the amount. Emphasis was laid on efficient tax collection machinery and stringent punishment for tax evasion.

Arthaśāstra

Arthaśāstra of Kauṭilya gives a detailed description of various tax rates and the measures for implementation of the basic tax policies. The relevant segments from this treatise are described below.

Methods of Tax Collection and Penalties for Violation of Rules

In Arthaśāstra there are detailed methods of tax collection and penalties for violation of each rule.

II/21/1: The Collector of Customs and Tolls should establish the customs house and the flag facing the east or the north in the vicinity of the big gates (of the city).

II/21/2: The receivers of duty, four or five in number, should record in writing (details about) traders who have arrived in caravan, who they are, from what place, with how much merchandise and where the identity-pass (was issued) or the stamping was made.

II/21/3; II/21/4; II/21/5; II/21/6; II/21/7: see Chapter 6 above.

II/21/8: When it has been thrice proclaimed, he should give it to those who have sought it.

II/21/9: In case of competition among purchasers, the increase in price together with the duty shall go to the treasury.

II/21/10; II/21/11; II/21/12; II/21/13; II/21/14; II/21/15: see Chapter 6 above.

II/21/16: And for goods that have passed beyond the foot of the flag without the duty being paid, the fine is eight times the duty.

II/21/17: see Chapter 6 above.

II/21/18: Goods intended for marriage, marriage-gifts accompanying the bride, goods intended as gifts, goods required on the occasion of a sacrifice or a ceremony or a birth and goods used in various rituals like worship of the gods, tonsure rite, initiation for Veda study, hair-cutting rite, consecration for a vow and so on, should go duty-free.

II/21/19: For a (person) making a false declaration (in this respect) the punishment for theft (shall be imposed).

II/21/20: For the trader taking out a commodity for which duty has not been paid along with one for which duty has been paid, or carrying off a second (commodity) under one stamp after breaking open the package, forfeiture of the same and an equal amount as fine (shall be the punishment).

II/21/21: For the (trader) carrying off (goods of high value) from the customs house after securing acceptance of cowdung (cakes) or straw as the basis (for calculating duty), the highest fine for violence (shall be the punishment).

II/21/22: For the (trader) taking out any one of the unexportable articles, viz., weapons, armours, coats of mail, metals, chariots, jewels, grains and cattle, there shall be a fine as proclaimed as well as loss of the goods.

II/21/23: In case anyone of these is brought in, its sell (shall be effected) duty-free outside (the city gate) itself.

II/21/24: The frontier officer should charge a road cess of one *paṇa* and a quarter for a cart-load of goods, of one *paṇa* for a one-hoofed animal, of half a *paṇa* for cattle, of a quarter *paṇa* for small animals, of one *māṣaka* for a shoulder-load.

II/21/25: And he shall make good what is lost or stolen (on the way).

II/21/26: He should send on to the Superintendent a caravan from a foreign land after making investigation as to goods of high and low value and giving them an identity-pass and stamp (on the goods).

II/21/27: See Chapter 6 above.

II/21/28: In accordance with that information, the king should tell the Collector of Customs about the size of the caravan, in order to make his omniscience known.

II/21/29: Then the Collector, on meeting the caravan, should say, 'These are goods of high and low value belonging to such and such merchant. It should not be concealed. This is the king's power.'

II/21/30: For one concealing goods of low value the fine shall be eight times the duty, (for concealing) goods of high value, confiscation of everything (shall be the punishment).

II/21/31: He should cut out goods that are harmful to the country and that are worthless. He should make goods that are highly beneficial duty-free, also seeds that are rare.

Tax Rates for Various Commodities

Tax rates for dealers in different kinds of spirituous liquors, not produced in the state sector are to be determined in the following manner:

II/25/39: Dealers in goods not manufactured by the state shall pay a duty of five percent on *surā*, *medaka*, *ariṣṭa*, *madhu*, sour fruit juices, and sour liquors.

Prostitutes and their musical instruments (if imported from foreign countries) are to be taxed in the following manner:

II/27/27: (Prostitutes) who live by their beauty, shall pay per month (a tax) double the (normal) fee (charged by them).

II/27/26: Their musical instruments, when coming from foreign lands, shall be charged a fee per show of five *paṇas*.

Duties on other commodities are to be determined in the following manner:

II/22/3: On goods coming in (the duty shall be) one-fifth of the price.

II/22/4: Of flowers, fruits, vegetables, roots, bulbous roots, fruits of creepers, seeds, dried fish and meat, he should take one-sixth part (as duty).

II/22/5: Of conch-shells, diamonds, gems and necklaces of pearls and corals, he should make (a valuation) through men expert in the line, making an agreement with them as to the amount of work, time allowed and wages.

II/22/6: On *kṣauma*, *dukūla*, silk yarn, armours, yellow orpiment, red arsenic, antimony, vermilion, metals of various kinds and ores, on sandal-wood, aloe, spices, fermentation, and minor substances, on skins, ivory, bed-spreads, coverings and silk cloth, and on products of goats and rams, (the duty to be charged is) one-tenth part or one-fifteenth part.

II/22/7: On clothes, four-footed and two-footed creatures, yarn, cotton, perfumes, medicines, woods, bamboos, barks, leather goods and earthen-ware, and on grains, fats, sugars, salts, wine, cooked food and so on (the duty is) one-twentieth part or one twenty-fifth part.

II/22/8: To be received at the gate is one-fifth of the normal duty, or he should fix it with a concession in accordance with the benefit derived by the country.

Surcharges

II/16/10: One-sixteenth part is the surcharge in measure by capacity, one-twentieth part in measure by weighing, one-eleventh part of commodities sold by counting.

Tax Concessions for Foreign (Imported) Commodities

II/16/11: He should encourage the import of goods produced in foreign lands by (allowing) concessions.

II/16/12: And to those (who bring such goods) in ships or caravans, he should grant exemptions (from taxes) that would enable a profit (to be made by them).

Like Manusmṛti, Arthaśāstra of Kauṭilya also lays more emphasis on indirect taxes than on direct taxes. There are only some brief mentions about fixed taxes on villages.

To quote:

II/6/10: Price, share, surcharge, monopoly tax, fixed tax, manufacturing charge and penalty constitute the heads of income.

II/28/2: Villages on their shores and banks shall pay a fixed (tax).

There is, however, no indication about the exact nature, rates and methods of collection of these taxes. One thing is clear from the study of Arthaśāstra that Kauṭilya nowhere mentioned taxes on incomes (of individuals or corporations).

Regarding other aspects, too, the basic principles here are similar to that of Manusmṛti. Kauṭilya also opines that tax rates should not be too high or too low, they should not exert much pressure on a few persons generating disincentive, taxes should be collected from everybody whatever small be the amount. He, like Manu, also emphasized the necessity of an efficient tax collection machinery and stringent punishment for tax evasion.

Relevance for Modern India

One of the major aspects of tax policy of India is that the government endeavours to increase the share of direct taxes as compared to indirect taxes. Different tax reforms committees, especially the Raja Chelliah Committee 1991, also advised the government to do so (Dhingra, op. cit.: 869-76).

But this sort of reasoning is not tenable in the light of the findings from the ancient texts we have discussed above. Let us first see the exact nature of Indian tax structure since independence.

Since independence, the proportion of indirect taxes in India have always been higher in the total tax revenue as is clear from the following table.

Table 8.1

Proportion of Direct and Indirect Taxes in India's Tax Revenue

Year	*Percentage of Direct Taxes*	*Percentage of Indirect Taxes*
1950-51	43.7	56.3
1960-61	32.5	67.5
1987-88	15.2	84.4
1990-91	16.3	83.7
1997-98	25.2	75.4
2003-04	28.3	71.7

Source: Tata Services Limited: *Statistical Outline of India* 2003-04, *Economic Survey*, various issues; *Union Budget*, 2003-04

From Table 8.1 it can be seen that in spite of increase of the proportion of direct taxes since 1990-91, the indirect taxes are still dominant. The major direct taxes of the Central Government are: (i) Personal Income Tax, and (ii) Corporation Tax. The major indirect taxes are: (i) Central Excise Duty, and (ii) Customs Duty.

The major problems of the Indian tax structure are:

(i) High marginal tax rates, particularly, in case of personal and corporate income taxes, resulting in disincentives in all spheres and encouraging evasion. In recent years the marginal rates have been reduced considerably, but they are still high.

(ii) The Tax Department is characterized by widespread corruption and inefficiency. This, along with high tax rates results in widespread tax evasion leading to the generation of black money and parallel economy.

(iii) Cost of tax collection is very high and overall productivity of the tax structure is low. A considerable proportion of the tax paid by the citizens are being absorbed to maintain the tax collecting machinery, giving a low proportion of net return.

(iv) Coverage of the tax structure is very low in terms of the total population of the country.

For the solution of the above problems, we may get considerable help from the prescriptions of both Manusmṛti and Arthaśāstra of Kauṭilya. We have discussed above how both these texts advised the king to fix taxes in such a way that rates are neither too high nor too low. High rates generate disincentives to work and tendency to evade taxes while low rates result in loss of revenue. In both the texts we find detailed guidelines for employing competent and honest tax-officials, vigilance through spies to detect corruption and punishments when any corruption or negligence is detected. We may tone up our tax machinery by utilizing (may be in a modified form to suit the present day situations), the prescriptions of the ancient texts as regards efficiency of the tax collection machinery.

The most important aspect of the relevance of the ancient texts is connected with the direct tax vs. indirect tax debate. The Government of India still emphasizes on the necessity of increasing the proportion of revenue from the direct taxes, although most of the problems like low returns, high collection costs, evasions, inefficiency and corruption of tax officials etc., are more serious in case of direct taxes than that of indirect taxes. We have seen that both Manu and Kauṭilya laid more emphasis on indirect taxes. The reason may be that direct taxes discourage income earning and indirect taxes discourage spending. It is not difficult to understand why encouragement to national income earners and discouragement to spenders are desirable for the benefit of the country.

So an important lesson from the ancient texts is that the government should depend more on indirect taxes than on direct taxes, i.e. the present emphasis of the tax policy in India has to be reversed.

Fiscal Policy

An inexorable part of the tax policy is the fiscal policy. So it is also necessary to have a glimpse of the fiscal policy in Manusmṛti and Arthaśāstra of Kauṭilya, and their modern relevance.

Fiscal policy is associated with taxation and government expenditure. Nowadays the economic systems and therefore fiscal policy has become far more complicated than in ancient times. So the question arises whether the ancient Indian texts could be of any use as regards reforming our fiscal policy today. To examine this let us first examine the fiscal policy as delineated in the two important ancient Indian texts, viz., Manusmṛti and Arthaśāstra of Kauṭilya under consideration.

Manusmṛti

As regards fiscal policy, from Manusmṛti we get the following basic guidelines:

7/133: A king even though dying (for want of money) should not realize revenue from a Vedic scholar; and no Vedic scholar living in his kingdom should be (suffered to be) embarrassed with hunger.

8/170: No king, however indigent, shall take anything that ought not to be taken, nor shall he, however wealthy, decline taking that which he ought to take, be it ever so small.

8/171: In consequence of his taking what ought not to be taken, or of his refusing what ought to be received, a king will be accused of weakness and perish in this (world) and after death.

8/419: Let him daily look after the completion of undertakings, his beasts of burden, and carriages, (the collection of) his revenues and the disbursements, his mines and his treasury.

[see also **7/139** above]

The essence underlying the above extracts is that the king should pursue a fiscal policy, which strikes a balance between fulfillment of short-term requirements and long term sustainability.

Arthaśāstra

The basic guidelines for fiscal policy in the Arthaśāstra are detailed in the following extracts:

II/1/15: And he should grant to them favours and exemptions which would cause an increase in the treasury, (but) avoid such as would cause loss to the treasury.

II/1/16: For, a king with a small treasury swallows up the citizens and the country people themselves.

II/6/28: Thus, the wise (administrator) should fix the revenue and show an increase in income and decrease in expenditure and should remedy the opposite (of these).

II/9/13: He who causes loss of revenue consumes the property of the king.

II/9/15: He who procures double the (normal) revenue, consumes the country side.

II/12/37: The treasury has its source in the mines; from the treasury the army comes into being. With the treasury and the army, the earth is obtained with the treasury as its ornament.

VI/1/1: The king, the minister, the country, the fortified city, the treasury, the army and the ally are the constituent elements (of the state).

VI/1/10: Acquired lawfully by the ancestors or by oneself, consisting mostly of gold and silver, containing various kinds of big jewels and cash, (one) that would withstand a calamity even of a long duration in which there is no income – these are the excellences of a treasury.

[Also see ***ślokas*** **II/5/22** and **II/7/24-33** in **Chapter 5** of this study]

The above extracts clearly point out the importance of a resourceful treasury for the functioning of the state. Moreover, stress is laid on sound finance, measures to enhance and enrich the treasury and to generate surplus in the state budget. At the same time it is emphasized that revenue collection of the state should not harm the interests of the country and its people. Thus we see that Kauṭilya insists on a surplus budget and suggests measures to avoid deficits in the budget. This is in conformity with ancient Indian principles of sound fiscal management.

In Arthaśāstra of Kauṭilya also prescribes measures for mobilizing finance for situations of crisis (*āpada dharma*). From a close study of these prescriptions, it is found that at the time of crisis, pressure for collecting additional finance (whether ethical or apparently unethical) should be exerted on the well to do persons and not on the poor.

[For further details see **Book V, Chapter 2**]

Relevance for Modern India

In ancient India, fiscal policy of the government aimed at maintaining a surplus budget and, at the worst, a balanced budget. So, unlike in modern states, deliberate fiscal and budgetary deficits were always avoided in those days. In fact, in ancient India, existence of deficits in state finances and public borrowing were looked upon as weakness of the government. According to Aiyangar, ancient Indian financial methods differed from modern methods as in the former, because of limited sources of revenue (printing of paper currency was unknown in those days and borrowing was considered to be inimical to sound finance), state expenditure could never be permitted to exceed the revenue received (Aiyangar, 1949: 162-64).

We have already seen that Arthaśāstra of Kauṭilya insists on maintenance of surplus budget and prescribes specific measures to achieve this end.

[see ***ślokas*** **II/1/15, 16** and **II/9/13, 15** as quoted above].

In case of serious financial crisis of the state, Kauṭilya even suggests certain measures, which may appear to be unethical [see **Book V, Chapter 2** of Arthaśāstra].

Nowadays, for facilitating economic development, many countries have gone in for heavy fiscal and budgetary deficits covered by borrowing (both internal and external) and deficit financing (circulation of new paper notes). But if these deficits do not result in increase in investment and production, deficits are incurred to finance mainly the consumption expenditure of the state, and unproductive and wasteful expenditure cannot be controlled, this will lead to serious problems for the economy.

In fact, this is the bitter experience of India in recent years. Many economists consider the heavy budgetary and fiscal deficits and the mounting burden of internal and external debt as some of the major causes of recent economic crisis in India. In 2003-04, India's overall internal public debt stood at Rs.1,158,639 crore and foreign debt at Rs.60,931 crore (*Statistical Outline of India*, 2003-04: 206).

A substantial part of new borrowing (both internal and external) is used for the repayment of old debt along with interest. So, at this stage, lessons from the ancient Indian texts, especially,

Manusmṛti and Arthaśāstra of Kauṭilya, may be of much help for maintaining a sound finance.

References

Aiyangar, K.V. Rangaswami (1949): *Indian Cameralism, a Survey of Some Aspects* of *Arthaśāstra*, The Adyar Library, Madras.

Government of India: *Economic Survey*, Various issues.

Tata Services Limited: *Statistical Outline of India 2003-2004*.

9

Women's Property Rights

Women's Property (Strīdhana)

One of the most important issues for which ancient Indian literature has much relevance today is women's rights and empowerment. Nowadays, there is much talk about this issue. Even an International Women's Year and decade were observed. In India since independence, various showbiz measures for empowerment of women have been adopted, e.g., reservation for women in various jobs, legislative bodies etc. All these would come to naught unless measures are adopted for financial security of women, and sexual security of women is ensured by stringent punishments for sexual crime by men against women. In this chapter we shall take up the case of property rights and financial security of women in Manusmṛti and Arthaśāstra of Kauṭilya.

Manusmṛti

As regards women's property rights, the statements in Manusmṛti appear at first sight to be contradictory. The following *ślokas* clearly speak against any property right of women:

8/416: A wife, a son, and a slave, these three are declared to have no property; the wealth which they earn is (acquired) for him to whom they belong.

9/2: Day and night, women must be kept in dependence by the males (of) their (families), and, if they attach themselves to sensual enjoyments, they must be kept under one's control.

9/3: Her father protects (her) in childhood, her husband protects (her) in youth, and her sons protect (her) in old age; a woman is never fit for independence.

But, the following *ślokas* give a clear description of the legal properties of women, how they are to be acquired, legal restrictions on using (misusing) these properties, how and when they would lose the legal property rights, who will inherit these properties etc:

The inheritance of property by women is specified in the following *ślokas*:

9/131: But whatever may be the separate property of the mother, that is the share of the unmarried daughters alone.

9/192: But when the mother has died, all the uterine brothers and the uterine sisters shall equally divide the mother's estate.

The following *ślokas* describe the source and origin of woman's property, its specific characteristics under different forms of marriage, the procedure of its use and rules for its inheritance:

9/194: What (was given) before the (nuptial) fire, what (was given) on the bridal procession, what was given in token of love, and what was received from her brothers, mother, or father, that is called the six-fold property of a woman.

9/195: (Such property), as well as a gift subsequent and what was given (to her) by her affectionate husband, shall go to her offspring, (even) if she dies in the lifetime of her husband.

9/196: It is ordained that the property (of a woman married) according to the *Brāhma*, the *Daiva*, the *Ārṣa*, the *Gāndharva*, or the *Prājāpatya* rite (shall belong to) her husband alone, if she dies without issue.

9/197: But it is prescribed that the property which may have been given to (wife) on an *Āsura* marriage or (one of the) other (blamable marriages, shall go) to her mother and to her father, if she dies without issue.

9/198: Whatever property may have been given by her father to a wife (who has co-wives of different castes), that the daughter of the *Brāhmaṇī* (wife) shall take, or that (daughter's) issue.

9/199: Woman should never make a hoard from (the property of) their families which is common to many, nor from their own (husband's particular) property without permission.

9/200: The ornaments, which may have been worn by women during their husbands' lifetime, his heirs shall not divide; those who divide them become outcastes.

9/217: A mother shall obtain the inheritance of a son (who dies) without leaving issue, and, if the mother be dead, the paternal grandmother shall take the estate.

Under any circumstances, it is prescribed that the financial security of women is to be ensured, whether through women's own property or by the male members. This is also clear from the following *ślokas*:

9/74: A man who has business (abroad) may depart after securing a maintenance for his wife; for a wife, even though virtuous, may be corrupted if she be distressed by want of subsistence.

9/75: If (the husband) went on a journey after providing (for her), the wife shall subject herself to restraints in her daily life; but if he departed without providing (for her), she may subsist by blameless manual work.

The following *ślokas* describe when and how a woman loses her property rights:

9/77: For one year let a husband bear with a wife who hates him; but after (the lapse of) a year let him deprive her of her property and cease to cohabit with her.

9/92: A maiden who chooses for herself, shall not take with her any ornaments, given by her father or her mother, or her brothers; if she carries them away, it will be theft.

The apparent contradiction in Manusmṛti about women's property rights may be resolved in the following manner. Manu considered that women's property rights and financial security must be ensured but all these should be under the strict guidance of the males. This standpoint of Manu springs from his apprehension of the frailty and fickle mindedness (emotional instability) of women, so that they are likely to misuse property if left on their own. It may be because of certain inherent shortcomings of women in general (irrespective of time and space) or the specific character of women in those days but it is quite clear that Manu considered it justified and necessary to impose certain restrictions on the freedom of women as regards their property rights for the benefit of both the women concerned and the society as a whole.

Arthaśāstra

In Arthaśāstra of Kauṭilya, as in many other ancient Indian texts, the basis of financial security to married women was *strīdhana* (woman's property). It consisted of landed property, jewellery, and money sufficient for maintenance of the married woman and her children. The funds were to be provided by the husband, the relatives of the husband and that of the woman who is to be married. The amount of the fund depended on the financial capabilities of the donors involved and the existing custom; but it should at least be sufficient to cover the subsistence of the woman and her children in case her husband dies, remarries or abandons her for no fault on her part. Maintenance of *strīdhana* was a legal compulsion and its violation was subject to punishment. The state had to enforce the observance of the rules pertaining to this financial arrangement.

The following excerpt from Kauṭilya's Arthaśāstra would corroborate the above observation:

III/2/14: Maintenance and ornaments constitute woman's property.

III/2/15: Maintenance is an endowment of a maximum of two thousand (*paṇas*); as to ornaments there is no limit.

The woman can use the fund (when the husband is still there) under the following situations (and the husband may also use the fund under certain situations):

To quote:

III/2/16: It is not an offence for the wife to use that for the maintenance of her sons and daughters-in-law or if no provision is made when (the husband is) away on a journey, (or) for the husband (to use it) for taking steps against robbers, diseases, famine (and other) dangers and for religious acts, or for the couple (to use it) jointly when they have begotten a son and a daughter.

The husband may, however, use the fund in the above cases only when the marriage had been a pious one.

To quote:

III/2/17: And if it has been used for three years, the (wife) shall not question, in the case of the pious marriages.

III/2/18: If used in the *Gāndharva* and *Āsura* marriages, the (husband) shall be made to return both with interest, if used in the *Rākṣasa* and *Paiśāca* marriages, he shall pay (the penalty for) theft.

Property Rights of the Widow without Remarriage

If a widow does not remarry, she would enjoy 'woman's property' until her dying day.

To quote:

III/2/19: When the husband is dead, the (widow), if desirous of leading a life of piety, shall forthwith receive the endowment and ornaments and the remainder of the dowry.

III/2/33: A (widow) without sons, remaining faithful to her husband's bed, shall use her woman's property in the proximity of elders, till the end of her life.

III/2/34: For, a woman's property is meant for calamities.

After remarriage the widow generally forfeits her rights to woman's property earned in the earlier marriage. However, a widow without sons may use this property for religious purposes alone.

To quote:

III/2/20: If, after receiving (these), she marries again, she shall be made to return both with interest.

III/2/26: A (widow) remarrying shall forfeit what was given her by her (late) husband.

III/2/27: She shall use it if desirous of a pious life.

A widow with sons always forfeits woman's property (from earlier marriage) after remarriage. She can use this property only for the maintenance and benefit of the sons.

To quote:

III/2/28: If a (widow) who has sons marries again, she shall forfeit her woman's property.

III/2/29: The sons, however, shall receive that woman's property.

III/2/30: Or, if she remarries for the maintenance of her sons, she shall augment (the woman's property) for the sake of the sons.

III/2/31: The (woman) shall settle on sons born (to her) from many husbands her woman's property as given by the respective fathers.

III/2/32: A (widow) marrying again shall settle on her sons her woman's property even when she is entitled to do what she pleases with it.

If a widow, without children, remarries in order to have children and a family, she may be permitted to enjoy woman's property if remarriage is done according to the likes of the earlier father-in-law's family.

To quote:

III/2/21: If, however, she is desirous of having a family, she shall receive, at the time of remarriage, what was given to her by her father-in-law and her (late) husband.

III/2/23: If she remarries against the wishes of her father-in-law, she shall forfeit what was given her by her father-in-law and her (late) husband.

The wife can abandon the husband and still enjoy woman's property in the following cases:

III/2/48: A husband, who has become degraded or gone to a foreign land or has committed an offence against the king or is dangerous to her life or has become an outcast or even an impotent one may be abandoned.

Remarriage of Women in Case of Short Absence of Husband

Kauṭilya clearly specifies the period for which a woman is to wait (to be permitted to remarry if she likes to do so) in case of short absence of husband for various castes and under various circumstances.

To quote:

III/4/24: The wives of a *Śūdra*, a *Vaiśya*, a *Kṣatriya* and a *Brāhmaṇa*, who are away on a short journey, shall wait for a period (of one year) increased successively by one year, if they have not borne children, for one year more, if they have borne children.

III/4/25: Those who are provided for (shall wait) for double the period.

III/4/26: The trustees shall maintain those unprovided for, kinsmen for four or eight years after that.

III/4/27: Thereafter, they shall release (them) after taking back according as they had given.

III/4/28: The (wife) shall wait for a *Brāhmaṇa* who is away studying, for ten years if she has no child, for twelve if she has a child, for a royal servant (she shall wait) till the end of her life.

III/4/29: And if she bears a child from a man of the same *varṇa*, she shall not incur blame.

III/4/30: Or, when the affluence of the family has disappeared, she, being released by the trustees, may marry again as she desires, or when she is in distress, for the sake of livelihood.

III/4/31: After a pious marriage, the maiden shall wait for her husband who has gone away without informing her, for seven periods if no news is heard about him, for one year if news is heard.

III/4/32: If he has gone away after informing her, she shall wait for five periods when no news is heard, for ten if news is heard.

III/4/33: If he had paid only a part of the dowry, she shall wait for three periods if there is no news, seven periods if there is news about him.

III/4/34: If he had paid the dowry (in full), (she shall wait) for five periods if there is no news, ten if there is news.

III/4/35: After that, she may remarry as she desires, with the permission of the judges.

III/4/36: 'For, frustration of the period is destruction of sacred duty', says Kauṭilya.

Remarriage of Women in Case of Long Absence of Husband

Kauṭilya also specifies the period for which a woman is to wait (to be permitted to remarry if she likes to do so) in case of long absence of husband.

To quote:

III/4/37: The wife of a (man) who has gone away on a long journey or has become a wandering monk or is dead shall wait for seven periods, for one year if she has borne children.

Conditions for Remarriage if the Husband does not Return in Time

If the husband does not return after the stipulated period and the woman is willing to marry, she can marry only certain specified relations of the husband. Otherwise, the marriage would not be recognized by law and considered as adultery.

To quote:

III/4/38: After that she may approach (for marriage) a full brother of the husband.

III/4/39: If there are many (such brothers, she should approach) one who is proximate (to the husband), one who is pious, one capable of maintaining her, or the youngest if without a wife.

III/4/40: In the absence of these, even one who is not a full brother, a *sapiṇḍa* or a member of the family who is near.

III/4/42: In case she marries setting aside these heirs of her husband, (or) in case she has a lover, the lover, the woman, the bestower (of the woman) and the man who marries her receive the penalty for adultery.

Inheritance of Women's Property

After the death of a woman her woman's property would be inherited by her sons and daughters (whether the husband is still alive or dead). In the absence of children, the husband, if alive, would receive a part of it and the other parts would be shared by the respective contributors.

To quote:

III/2/36: If a woman dies while her husband is living, her sons and daughters shall divide her woman's property among themselves, daughters (only) if she had no sons, in the absence of these the husband (shall receive it).

III/2/37: The dowry, the post-marriage gifts and other things given by her relations, the relations shall receive.

Financial Obligations of Men to his Wife and Other Dependents

In the Arthaśāstra, Kauṭilya prescribes that it would be obligatory for a man to provide for the upkeep of his wife and children as well as parents, minor brothers, and unmarried and widowed sisters. In case he fails to discharge duties in this regard, he will be fined. He is not obliged to do these duties if anyone mentioned above (except mother), become an outcaste. It appears that he is to maintain his mother even if she becomes an outcaste.

To quote:

II/1/28: If a person with means does not maintain his children and wife, his father and mother, his brothers who have not come of age, and his unmarried and widowed sisters, a fine of twelve *paṇas* (shall be imposed), except when these have become outcaste, with the exception of the mother.

A person desiring to renounce family life to become an ascetic can do so only after he makes adequate provisions for the wife and children. And, nobody should be permitted to induce a woman to renounce family life.

To quote:

II/1/29: If one renounces home (to become an ascetic) without providing for his sons and wife, the lowest fine for violence (shall be imposed), also if one induces a woman to renounce home.

Relevance for Modern India

In recent years, there has been much emphasis on the empowerment of women in India. Measures like reservation of seats for women in various public bodies like the panchayat*s*, the State Assemblies, the Parliament etc., have been undertaken. There are also legal measures against oppression of married women in the husband's family. But still there are no specific measures to ensure financial security of women, without which all other measure are likely to become meaningless. We have seen from the discussion above that financial security of women was given top priority in Manusmṛti and Arthaśāstra of Kauṭilya. Particularly, the concept of *Strīdhana* (woman's property) gives us an idea how financial security of married women till her dying day could be ensured. In fact, one undesirable aspect of western culture on our society in recent years is the inducement to disintegrate the family system, which is the building block of Indian society. So, the culture ensuring permanency of marriage is to be encouraged to obviate the harmful influence of nihilistic western culture. In this respect assurance of women's financial security is an urgent necessity. The ancient concept of woman's property, if revived (in a modified form to suit the needs of modern society), is likely to play an important role in ensuring women's financial security. This is the most mention-worthy relevance of ancient texts as regards empowerment of women.

10

Division of Labour

Efficiency-based Division of Labour

Division of labour has gained much importance in the modern era. Originally, it started with the social division of labour under which each person adopted a separate profession since it was not possible for a person to produce all the goods and services he required. Each person worked according to his capability, and with the income thus earned he purchased from others all the requisites for his livelihood. In ancient India, this division of labour was looked upon as a part of the harmony of the universe and something ordained by the creator. From this standpoint, division of labour was based on the caste (*varṇa*) system.

But, at present, society has become more complicated and viewpoints regarding traditional castes have changed considerably. With the emergence of factory industries, division of labour has become more intense, as in an industrial establishment each person produces only a part of the total product. The nature of human activities, too have changed, multiplied and become more diverse and qualitatively different. Under this situation, it is almost impossible to revive the traditional caste system as such. The problem has become more complicated with the increase in the degree of intercourse with foreign countries as a consequence of the revolutionary changes in transport and communications in recent years. So, it would be interesting to see if the caste-based division of labour in ancient India has any relevance for modern India at all. Here, we may briefly mention that although the ancient system as such may not be appropriate for India today, the essence of the ancient system is likely to be of much significance. Before going into that matter let us have a glimpse of the ancient system of caste-based division of labour as prescribed in Manusmṛti and Arthaśāstra of Kauṭilya.

Manusmṛti

Manu opines that the creator has prescribed certain general tasks for the human race for different ages. But He also assigned specific duties to specific classes of people. According to Manu, *Brāhmaṇas* originated from the mouth, *Kṣatriyas* from the arms, *Vaiśyas* from the thighs, and *Śūdras* from the feet of the creator. So, they have different functions in all the ages.

To quote:

1/86: In the *Kṛta* age the chief (virtue) is declared to be (the performance of) austerities, in the *Tretā* divine knowledge, in the *Dvāpara* (the performance of) sacrifices, while in the *Kali,* liberality alone.

1/87: But in order to protect his universe He, the most resplendent one, assigned separate (duties and) occupations to those who sprang from his mouth, arms, thighs, and feet.

Under normal situations, the functions of the four castes as mentioned above, are the following. In brief, duties of the *Brāhmaṇas* are associated with the study of the Vedas and performance of the religious rites; that of the *Kṣatriyas* are associated with war and defence of the country; that of the *Vaiśyas* are associated with trade and agriculture and that of the *Śūdras* to serve the three upper classes.

1/102: In order to clearly settle his duties and those of the other (castes) according to their order, wise Manu sprung from the self-existent, composed these institutes (of the Sacred Law).

1/88: To *Brāhmaṇas* he assigned teaching and studying (the Veda), sacrificing for their own benefit and for others, giving and accepting (of alms).

1/89: The *Kṣatriya* he commanded to protect the people, to bestow gifts, to offer sacrifices, to study (the Veda), and to abstain from attaching himself to sensual pleasures.

1/90: The *Vaiśya* to tend cattle, to bestow gifts, to offer sacrifices, to study (the Veda), to trade, to lend money, and to cultivate land.

8/410: (The king) should order a *Vaiśya* to trade, to lend money, to cultivate the land, or to tend cattle, and a *Śūdra* to serve the twice-born class.

1/91: One occupation only the lord prescribed to the *Śūdra*, to serve meekly even these (other) three castes.

9/334: But to serve *Brāhmaṇas* (who are) learned in the Vedas, householders, and famous (for virtue) is the highest duty of a *Śūdra*, which leads to beatitude.

Manu specifies six major functions of the *Brāhmaṇa*, out of which only three are for his livelihood. He cannot earn means of livelihood from the other three, viz., teaching, studying and sacrificing for himself.

To quote:

10/75: Teaching, studying, sacrificing for himself, sacrificing for others, making gifts and receiving them are the six acts (prescribed) for a *Brāhmaṇa*.

10/76: But among the six acts (ordained) for him three are his means of subsistence, (viz.) sacrificing for others, teaching, and accepting gifts from pure men.

Kṣatriyas and *Vaiśyas* are forbidden from three acts of the *Brāhmaṇa*, viz., teaching, sacrificing for others and acceptance of gifts.

To quote:

10/77: (Passing) from the *Brāhmaṇas* to the *Kṣatriya*, three acts (incumbent on the former) are forbidden, (viz.) teaching, sacrificing for others, and, thirdly, the acceptance of gifts.

10/78: The same are likewise forbidden to a *Vaiśya*, that is a settled rule; to Manu, the lord of the creatures (*Prajāpati*), has not prescribed for (men of) those two (castes).

Among the activities prescribed for the *Kṣatriyas* and the *Vaiśyas*, means of subsistence for *Kṣatriyas* is only military profession, and that for the *Vaiśyas* are agriculture, trade and animal husbandry.

To quote:

10/79: To carry arms for striking and for throwing (is prescribed) for *Kṣatriyas* as a means of subsistence; to trade, (to rear) cattle, and agriculture for *Vaiśyas*; but their duties are liberality, the study of the Veda, and the performance of sacrifices.

In the following *ślokas*, Manu specifies the most important activity (among all the permissible activities) of each caste.

10/80: Among the several occupations the most commendable are teaching the Veda for a *Brāhmaṇa*, protecting (the people) for a *Kṣatriya*, and trade for a *Vaiśya*.

10/123: The service of *Brāhmaṇas* alone is declared (to be) an excellent occupation for a *Śūdra*; for whatever else besides this he may perform will bear him no fruit.

These duties of the four castes, according to Manu, have been defined rigidly by the creator.

To quote:

10/97: It is better (to discharge) one's own (appointed) duty incompletely than to perform completely that of another; for he who lives according to the law of another (caste) is instantly excluded from his own.

1/30: As at the change of the seasons each season of its own accord assumes its distinctive marks, even so corporeal beings (resume in new births) their (appointed) course of action.

In each succeeding age, because of the change in the nature of activities due to change in the complexities of human society, the detailed nature of activities of each caste changed, but in essence, they remained the same (at least in spirit) as originally ordained by the creator. This implies that whatever the outward form or name of specific activities, the assigned activities of each class remained unchanged in terms of degree of virtue or sin.

To quote:

1/28: But to whatever course of action Lord at first appointed each (kind of beings), that alone it has spontaneously adopted in each succeeding creation.

1/29: Whatever he assigned to each at the (first) creation, noxiousness or harmlessness, gentleness or ferocity, virtue or sin, truth or falsehood, that clung (afterwards) spontaneously to it.

Manu opines that if a person belonging to any caste relinquishes his assigned duties and adopts some forbidden duty, will be degenerated, unless he is compelled to do so by unavoidable pressure of circumstances.

To quote;

12/70: But (men of the four) castes who have relinquished without the pressure of necessity their proper occupation, will become the servants of *Dasyus*, after migrating into despicable bodies.

It appears that Manu considered division of labour according to castes was hereditary.

10/5: In all castes (*varṇa*) those (children) only which are begotten in the direct order on wedded wives, equal (in castes and married as) virgins, are to be considered as belonging to the same caste (as their fathers).

10/6: Sons, begotten by twice-born men on wives of the next lower castes, they declare to be similar (to their fathers, but) blamed on account of the fault (inherent) in their mothers.

Under financial stringency, and inability to subsist by his own proper activities, a *Brāhmaṇa* may adopt a *Kṣatriya's* profession or even a *Vaiśya's* profession.

10/81: But a *Brāhmaṇa*, unable to subsist by his peculiar occupations just mentioned, may live according to the law applicable to *Kṣatriyas*; for the latter is next to him in rank.

10/82: If it be asked, 'How shall it be, if he cannot maintain himself by either (of these occupations?' the answer is), he may adopt a *Vaiśya's* mode of life, employing himself in agriculture and rearing cattle.

Even under financial crisis, a *Brāhmaṇa*, or a *Kṣatriya* should avoid agricultural activities, and trade in certain articles as specified by Manu.

10/83: But a *Brāhmaṇa*, or a *Kṣatriya*, living by a *Vaiśya's* mode of subsistence, shall carefully avoid (the pursuit of) agriculture, (which causes) injury to many beings and depends on others.

10/84: (Some) declare that agriculture is something excellent, (but) that means of subsistence is blamed by the virtuous; (for) the wooden (implement) with iron point injures the earth and (the beings) living in the earth.

10/85: But he who, through a want of means of subsistence, gives up the strictness with respect to his duties, may sell, in order to increase his wealth, the commodities sold by *Vaiśyas*, making (however) the (following) exceptions.

10/86: He must avoid (selling) condiments of all sorts, cooked food and sesamum, stones, salt, cattle, and human (beings).

10/87: All dyed cloth, as well as cloth made of hemp, or flax, or wool, even though they be not dyed, fruit, roots, and (medical) herbs.

10/88: Water, weapons, poison, meat, *soma*, and perfumes of all kinds, fresh milk, honey, sour milk, clarified butter, oil, wax, sugar, *Kuśa*-grass.

10/89: All beasts of the forest, animals with fangs or tusks, birds, spirituous liquor, indigo, lac, and all one-hoofed beasts.

10/90: But he who subsists by agriculture, may at pleasure sell unmixed sesamum grains for sacred purposes, provided he himself has grown them and has not kept them long.

In financial distress, a *Vaiśya* may adopt a *Śūdra's* profession, but not a *Brāhmaṇa's*. A *Śūdra* may subsist serving a *Kṣatriya* or a *Vaiśya* if he is unable to find adequate jobs to serve the *Brāhmaṇas*. Even if he does not find that, he may subsist by handicrafts and various arts which are likely to come to the service of the upper castes. But in no case he would be permitted to adopt the profession of higher castes. If any person, belonging to a lower caste, adopts the profession of a higher caste, he would be punished by the king.

To quote:

10/98: A *Vaiśya* who is unable to subsist by his own duties, may even maintain himself by a *Śūdra's* mode of life, avoiding (however) acts forbidden (to him), and he should give it up, when he is able (to do so).

10/121: "If a *Śūdra*, (unable to subsist by serving *Brāhmaṇas*) seeks livelihood, he may serve *Kṣatriyas*, or he may also seek to maintain himself by attending on a wealthy *Vaiśya*.

10/99; 10/100: see Chapter 4 above.

10/96: A man of low caste who through covetousness lives by the occupations of a higher one, the king shall deprive him of his property and banish him.

Manu opines that a *Śūdra* cannot do anything that degrades him in caste as there is no lower caste than his. He is also forbidden to undertake various sacred rites meant for the upper castes.

To quote:

10/126: A *Śūdra* cannot commit an offence, causing loss of caste (*pātaka*), and he is not worthy to receive the sacraments; he has no right to (fulfill) the sacred law (of the Aryans, yet) there is no prohibition against (his fulfilling certain portions of) the law.

Manu also prescribes for prohibition of wealth accumulation by a *Śūdra*, because of his vile mentality, a wealthy *Śūdra* is likely to cause trouble for the *Brāhmaṇas*.

To quote:

10/129: No collection of wealth must be made by a *Śūdra*, even though he be able (to do it); for a *Śūdra* who has acquired wealth, gives pain to *Brāhmaṇa*.

Manu is of the view that observance of the specified duties by people belonging to the four castes will benefit all of them.

To quote:

10/130: The duties of the four castes (*varṇa*) in times of distress have thus been declared, and if they perform them well, they will reach the most blessed state.

Mixed Castes

Besides the four major castes many mixed castes originated because of inter-caste marriages. Manu defined the functions of these mixed castes also. These mixed castes went on ramifying with increased branches with the advancement of time. For example, among the four basic castes marriages of lower-caste males with upper-caste females may create six inferior castes. From these six sub-castes, further 120 (5×4×3×2×1) sub-castes may be generated by inter-caste marriages and so on. As the number of these sub-castes went on increasing it became difficult to specify the appropriate duties of each new castes. This led to disharmony and chaos in the social fabric.

Some of the sub-castes as mentioned by Manu are given below [for detail see ***ślokas*** **10/32-10/52** of Manusmṛti].

Āhiṇḍika, Ambaṣṭhas, Andhra, Antyāvasāyin, Āyogava, Caṇḍāla, Dāsa, Dasyu, Dhigvaṇas, Kaivarta, Kārāvara, Kṣttṛs, Kuňkus, Madgus, Māgadhas, Maitreyaka, Mārgava, Meda,

Niṣāda, Pāṇḍusopāka, Pukkasa, Sairandhra, Sopāka, Sūtas, Ugras, Vaideha, Vaidehaka, Veṇas.

The general conclusion from the above discussion is that division of labour according to Manu was based on heredity and a rigidly defined caste system. This was necessary to avoid chaos and to bring about harmonious and orderly progress of the society. Basically, the essence of the caste system was that division of the society into the four major castes should be on the basis of inherent qualities. It is quite natural that with the progress of society the number of castes went on multiplying, generating complications and chaos. So it was no longer possible to determine castes solely on the basis of merits. In such a situation, the easiest way to determine castes was by birth. At the initial stage this did not create much problem as specific attributes are likely to be inherited to some extent and family atmosphere and training from the very childhood was likely to make a person considerably efficient in his family profession. Thus, in Manusmṛti we find that castes were mainly determined by birth. In Arthaśāstra also we find similar view regarding division of labour on the basis of caste or *varṇas*. These are discussed below.

Arthaśāstra

Like Manu, Kauṭilya also defines division of labour on the basis of division of the society into four major castes, viz., *Brāhmaṇa*, *Kṣatriya*, *Vaiśya* and *Śūdra*. The functions of these four castes are almost the same as in Manusmṛti.

I/3/4: The law laid down in this Vedic lore is beneficial, as it prescribes the respective duties of the four *varṇas* and the four stages of life.

I/3/5: The special duties of the *Brāhmaṇa* are: studying, teaching, performing sacrifices for self, officiating at other people's sacrifices, making gifts and receiving gifts.

I/3/6: Those of the *Kṣatriya* are: studying, performing sacrifices for self, making gifts, living by (the profession of) arms and protecting beings.

I/3/7: Those of the *Vaiśya* are: studying, performing sacrifice for self, making gifts, agriculture, cattle-rearing and trade.

I/3/8: Those of the *Śūdra* are: service of the twice-born, engaging in an economic calling (viz., agriculture, cattle-rearing and trade) and the profession of the artisan and the actor.

The functions of the first three castes are the same here as prescribed by Manu. But as regards the functions of the *Śūdra*, Kauṭilya differs a bit from Manu as he includes agriculture as one of the professions for the *Śūdras*. (Manu considers this to be a profession exclusively of the *Vaiśyas*).

To quote:

II/1/2: He should cause villages to be settled consisting mostly of *Śūdra* agriculturists, with a minimum of one hundred families and a maximum of five hundred families, with boundaries extending over one *krośa* or two *krośas*, (and) affording mutual protection.

Kauṭilya also mentions some specific duties for people in different walks of life, e.g., householders, Vedic students, forest-dwelling and wandering ascetics etc.

I/3/9: Those of the householder are: earning his living in accordance with his own special duty, marrying into families of the same caste but not of the same *gôtra*, approaching the wife during the period, worship of the gods, manes and guests, making gifts to dependents and eating what is left over (after the others have eaten).

I/3/10: Those of the student of the Veda are: studying the Veda, tending the (sacred) fires and (ceremonial) bathing, keeping the vow of living on alms only, residing till the end of his life with the preceptor or, in his absence, with the preceptor's son or with a fellow-student.

I/3/11: Those of the forest-anchorite are: observing celibacy, sleeping on bare ground, wearing matted locks and an antelope-skin, worship of the (sacred) fires and (ceremonial) bathing, worshipping the gods, manes and guests and living on forest produce (only).

I/3/12: Those of the wandering ascetic are: having full control over the senses, refraining from all active life, being without any possessions, giving up all attachment to worldly ties, keeping the vow of begging alms, not residing in one place and in the forest, and observing external and internal cleanliness.

Kauṭilya opines that one should stick to his own assigned duties and this will lead to success and happiness in this world as well as beyond this worldly life. On the other hand, violation of this would lead to mixture of duties leading to chaos and confusion. To quote:

I/3/14: (The observance of) one's own special duty leads to heaven and to endless bliss.

I/3/15: In case of its transgression, people would be exterminated through (the) mixture (of duties and castes).

Kauṭilya considers this division of duties on the basis of castes as sacred, and entrusts the duty of preserving it with the king.

I/3/16: Therefore, the king should not allow the special duties of the (different) beings to be transgressed (by them); for, ensuring adherence to (each one's) special duty, he finds joy after death as well as in this life.

Kauṭilya describes the benefits of preserving the division of labour according to prescription in the following manner.

I/3/17: For people, among whom the bounds of the Aryan rule of life are fixed, among whom the *varṇas* and the stages of life are securely established and who are guarded by the three Vedas, prosper, do not perish.

Kauṭilya mentions various mixed castes and their specific functions in sloka **III/7**. Many of his mixed castes are common to

Manu and many are different. This is simply because the two texts were written in different time periods, with differences in caste composition of the society.

On the whole the approach of Arthaśāstra of Kauṭilya towards division of labour is guided by the principle of order and harmony in the society and in this respect it reflects the same basic view point as in Manusmṛti.

Relevance for Modern India

Division of labour and choice of profession in ancient India (as discussed above) were based on heredity and the rules of four *varṇas* (castes) and *āśramas* (stages of life). Children belonging to a particular caste or sub-caste were trained for the appropriate job prescribed for the caste/sub-caste from the very childhood. This ensured efficiency, work culture and overall harmony of the society and the economic system. But, in modern India, there is no such coherent and systematic rule for division of labour and choice of professions. Anybody can select any profession even if he does not have any aptitude for doing so. In most of the cases, selection of a person for a job is based on factors other than individual education, competence or efficiency. Political and social connections, interests of political parties, trade unions etc. also play their roles while selecting a person for job. All these have resulted in chaos, inefficiency, lack of work culture and have instilled imbalance and disharmony into the fabric of the society and the economic system in India today. In this context, we may learn from the ancient Indian texts and examine if we could re-introduce some system like the ancient Indian caste system (may be in a modified form) for choice of professions and division of labour.

However, it is not possible to revive the ancient system of caste-based division of labour as it is. That is also not desirable today since the social system of India has changed considerably in the course of evolution, rendering it unsuitable for the ancient system. Many ancient castes still exist today in various parts of India, but only in name. The nature of activities of persons belonging to these castes hardly corresponds with the ancient specifications. There have emerged thousands of mixed castes, which were completely non-existent in ancient times. So the question arises what lessons we are likely to learn from the ancient texts as regards division of labour. In this regard we must not consider the prescriptions in ancient texts at their face value, but should get down to the essence of those specifications.

The essence of the prescriptions in this regard in ancient texts is that professions should be chosen on the basis of aptitude. Each person adopting a particular profession should stick to the profession selected and should receive perfect training in it, once it is properly chosen. In this respect, we also cannot deny the role of heredity in selection of professions. In fact, in many cases professions are chosen this way even today.

Heredity in many cases attributes some inherited qualities from the very birth, and training facilities are also the best if one selects his profession by this criterion. But this cannot be a hard and fast rule in the modern world. A person who has no aptitude for his father's profession but has aptitude for some other profession, ought to get the opportunity to adopt the latter. There should, however, be a proper method of screening the aptitude of a person before permitting him to enter into some profession. Moreover, there should be rigorous and appropriate theoretical and practical training for each person entering a particular profession, and there should be rigid restrictions on frequent change of professions. These are the relevant things that we may adopt from the essence of the prescriptions of the ancient texts as regards division of labour.

11

The Procedure of Making a Good Ruler

Role of Selfless Persons to Control the Rulers and Politicians

Ancient Indian texts entrusted the king with the task of maintaining order and rule of 'dharma' in society. The king as the supreme ruler had to have appropriate qualities to rule, regulate and maintain harmony and order, and to accomplish this, he was authorized to punish the miscreants with the help of the rod of punishment (*daṇḍa*). Under a perfect ruler, peace, harmony and prosperity prevail in the kingdom. An incompetent or corrupt king, on the other hand, would bring about disorder and destruction of himself, his kingdom and the subjects. So, it was an urgent necessity to train the king in a proper way from his very childhood.

Both Manusmṛti and Arthaśāstra of Kauṭilya prescribe procedures to make a proper ruler. This is an important aspect, which may be of much relevance for India today. One of the most serious problems in India since independence is the prevalence of incompetent and corrupt politicians in all the political parties aspiring to rule at various levels of government (Centre, states, local bodies etc). So, it would be of much help for governance in

Modern India if we could emulate some prescriptions from these texts to develop honest and competent politicians. Let us first discuss the methods prescribed for this purpose in Manusmṛti and Arthaśāstra of Kauṭilya.

Manusmṛti

Qualities of an Appropriate King

To be a good ruler, the king should regulate his lifestyle in a proper way. Only then would he have the right and power to rule the country and apply the rod of punishment to the miscreants. He should be intelligent, free from addiction to vices, cultured, upright, should have self-control and should respect the elders and the *Brāhmaṇas*. He should have proper education (of the Vedas, politics, history, agriculture, spiritual science etc.) and he should protect his subjects with zeal.

To quote:

7/30: It (the rod) cannot be rightly employed by a king who is without friends, foolish, avaricious, uncultured and addicted to sensuous objects.

7/31: It can be employed by a king who is pure (in monetary matters), true to his promise, intelligent, backed by friends and a follower of the *śāstriya* path.

7/32: In his own kingdom he should be of upright conduct, to his enemies he should be of rigorous punishment, to his natural friends he should be sincere, and towards the *Brāhmaṇas*, he should be forgiving.

7/33: Of a king of such a conduct, the fame spreads in the world, like a drop of oil on water.

7/34: But of a king who has not subdued himself and is the opposite of the one described before, the fame (which he has already possessed) shrinks in the world, like a drop of ghee on water.

7/35: Of all the *varṇas* (castes) and of all the *aśramas* (stages of life) attending to their own duties in due order, the king has been created (by *Brāhmaṇas*) as the protector.

7/37: A king getting up in the morning, should honour the *Brāhmaṇas* matured in the knowledge of the three Vedas and learned in polity, and should abide by their advice.

7/38: A king should honour the *Brāhmaṇas* advanced in age etc., learned in the Vedas, and pure externally and internally. For, one, who honours the elders, is worshipped even by demons.

In the following *ślokas*, Manu stresses the importance of self-control for the king, cites examples of past kings ruined for lack of it and also those who prospered by virtue of the attribute of self-control.

To quote:

7/39: A king, who is already controlled in his senses, should always learn self-control from them. For a king who is self-controlled, does not perish.

7/40: A good many kings, though provided with resources, have perished through want of self-control and a good many of them, though doomed to forest life (i.e., though without resources), have gained kingdoms through self-control.

7/41: Vena, Nahuṣa, Sudāh, son of Pijavana, Sumukha and Nimi – these kings perished through want of self-control.

7/42: On the other hand, Prithu got the kingdom through self-control, so also Manu. And (through self-control) did Kubera attain mastery over wealth, and Gādhi's son (Viśwāmitra) the state of a *Brāhmaṇa*.

The king should have proper educational training in Vedas, politics, logic, spiritual sciences and economic pursuits like agriculture.

To quote:

7/43: He should practice the three Vedas from those versed in the same and should learn the eternal politics as well as logic, spiritual science and agriculture etc. from men versed in those subjects.

In most of the cases uncontrolled senses lead a person to commit sins. So the king should give utmost attention to control the senses. He should also be careful about controlling the vices generating from, greed, desire and anger.

To quote:

7/44: The king should devote his attention day and night to the conquering of the senses. For a king with his senses controlled, is able to keep with his subjects under subjugation.

7/45: He should carefully shun the ten vices springing from desire and the eight vices springing from anger all of which ends in misery.

7/49: He should carefully conquer greediness which sages regard as the root of both these groups. Really both these groups spring from greed.

The above are the basic qualities of a king. Having armed with these qualities the king should protect his subjects with zeal as it is the basic duty of a *Kṣatriya*.

To quote:

7/142: Having thus arranged the entire details of his own affairs (relating to government), he should protect his subjects with zeal and care.

7/144: The highest duty of a *Kṣatriya* is to protect his subjects.

The king, for his proper guidance and training, should select an appropriate *Brāhmaṇa*, and the priest of his family. So the responsibility of keeping the king on the path of virtue is to be entrusted with the *Brāhmaṇa*.

7/58: With the most distinguished among them, a learned *Brāhmaṇa*, the king should discuss the most important (hence confidential) affairs connected with the six measures of royal policy.

7/59: With full confidence the king should entrust all affairs to him. He should commence work after fully discussing it with him.

Routine of a Perfect King

The maintenance and preservation of the proper qualities of the king for discharging his duties in a proper way requires him to lead a disciplined lifestyle. Various aspects related to the administration of the country should be arranged in a harmonious and orderly fashion and each duty should be performed at their proper time as prescribed in the *ślokas* below.

7/145: Having risen in the last watch (of the night) and having performed the acts of purgation, having offered sacrifices into the fire and having worshipped the *Brāhmaṇas*, he should with a controlled mind enter the Assembly-hall possessed of auspicious signs.

7/146: Seated there he should receive and then dismiss all the subjects, and having dismissed all the subjects, he should deliberate with his ministers.

7/147: Having ascended the surface of a hill, or being in a room in private, or in a lonely forest, he should have deliberations without being observed by others.

7/216: Having thus deliberated on all these matters with his ministers, having taken physical exercise and having bathed at mid-day, he should enter the harem to eat his meal.

7/221: Having eaten his meal, he should spend his time in the harem in company with his wives, and having diverted himself at the proper time, he should again think of the affairs (of the state).

7/222: Adorned with his robes, he should inspect the troops as well as the conveyances, and all kinds of weapons, accoutrements and ornaments.

7/223-224: After having performed the evening ceremony, he should enter into the interior of another room, and there, properly armed, he should hear the reports of the secret spies, and then having dismissed them and being surrounded by females, he should enter the inner apartment to take his meal again.

7/225: Then being exhilarated by the sounds of music, he, after having taken some food, should retire for sleep and get up refreshed at the proper time.

7/226: The king when he is in good health, should (himself) observe these. But when indisposed, he should entrust all these to his (responsible) servants.

From the above *ślokas*, it is seen that the king had to be engaged in activities pertaining to the administration of the kingdom most of the time of the day. Only for a brief time period would he take his meals, meet calls of nature and spend time in the harem. At the end of the day's engagements, he would retire for sleep for a few hours and get up next morning to enter into another busy day.

Arthaśāstra

Education and Training of the King

To be competent enough to rule the country properly, the king should go through adequate education and training. The details of these are given in the following *ślokas*.

I/5/7: When the ceremony of tonsure is performed, the (prince) should learn the use of the alphabet and arithmetic.

I/5/8: When the initiation with the preceptor is performed, he should learn the three Vedas and philosophy from the learned, economics from the heads of departments (and) the science of politics from theoretical and practical exponents.

I/5/9: And (he should observe) celibacy till the sixteenth year.

I/5/10: Thereafter (should follow) the cutting of the hair and marriage for him.

I/5/11: And (he should have) constant association with elders in learning for the sake of improving his training, since training has its root in that.

The daily routine for education of the future king is to be found in the following extracts.

I/5/12: During the first part of the day, he should undergo training in the arts of (using) elephants, horses, chariots and weapons.

I/5/13: In the latter part, (he should engage) in listening to *Itihāsa*.

I/5/14: The Purāṇas, *Itivṛtta, Ākhyāyikā, Udāharaṇa, Dharmaśāstra* and *Arthaśāstra* – these constitute *Itihāsa.*

I/5/15: During the remaining parts of the day and the night, he should learn new things and familiarise himself with those already learnt, and listen repeatedly to things not learnt.

Importance of Continuous Study

I/5/16: For, from (continuous) study ensues a (trained) intellect, from intellect (comes) practical application, (and) from practical application (results) self-possession; such is the efficacy of sciences.

I/5/17: For, the king, trained in the sciences, intent on the discipline of the subjects, enjoys the earth (alone) without sharing it with any other (ruler), being devoted to the welfare of all beings.

Importance of Moral Education

Kauṭilya, however, is of opinion that general education and training are not enough to make a perfect king. Moral and ethical teachings are also necessary. He explains the importance and methods of moral training of a king with examples of downfall of many past kings, who used to violate one or more of the essential ethical norms for an ideal king, in the following manner.

First Kauṭilya reiterates the importance of having control over the senses.

To quote:

I/6/1: Control over the senses, which is motivated by training in the sciences, should be secured by giving up lust, anger, greed, pride, arrogance and fool-hardiness.

A contrary behaviour would bring about ruin of the king, whatever be his apparent power. In this regard Kauṭilya mentions how the different past kings (historical and mythical) perished for lack of control over senses.

To quote:

I/6/4: A king, behaving in a manner contrary to that, (and hence) having no control over his senses, quickly perishes, though he be ruler right up to the four ends of the earth.

I/6/5: For example, the Bhoja king Dāṇḍakya by name, entertaining a sinful desire for a *Brāhmaṇa* maiden, perished along with his kinsmen and kingdom; and (so did) Karāla, king of the Videhas.

I/6/6: Janamejaya, using violence against *Brāhmaṇas*, out of anger, (likewise perished); and (so did) Tālajaṅgha, (using violence) against the Bhṛgus.

I/6/7: Aila, extorting money from the four varṇas out of greed, (perished); and (so did) Ajavindu of the Sauvīras.

I/6/8: Rāvaṇa, not restoring the wife of another through pride, (perished); and (so did) Duryodhana (not returning) a portion of the kingdom.

I/6/9: Dambhodbhava, treating creatures with contempt out of arrogance, (perished); and (so did) Arjuna of the Haihayas.

I/6/10: Vātāpi, trying to assail Agastya, out of foolhardiness, (perished); and (so did) the clan Vṛṣṇis (trying to assail) Dvaipāyana.

So the king should have control over senses by conquering the six basic vices (lust, anger, greed, pride, illusion and jealously), and acquire wisdom from the elders to be fit for ruling the country.

To quote:

I/7/1: Therefore, by casting out the group of six enemies he should acquire control over senses, cultivate his intellect by association with elders, keep a watchful eye by means of spies, bring about security and well-being by (energetic) activity, maintain the observance of their special duties (by the subjects) by carrying out (his own) duties, acquire discipline by (receiving) instruction in the sciences, attain popularity by association with what is of material advantage and maintain (proper) behaviour by (doing) what is beneficial.

According to Kauṭilya, the ideal king should have perfect control over the senses. But this does not necessarily imply that the king should not at all indulge in material pleasures. In fact, Kauṭilya subscribes to the traditional Indian view that there should be a perfect balance of the *trivarga* (i.e., *dharma*, *artha* and *kāma*) in the life of the king, as is evident from the following *ślokas*.

I/7/3: He should enjoy sensual pleasure without contravening his spiritual good and material well-being; he should not deprive himself of pleasures.

I/7/4: Or, (he should devote himself) equally to the three goals of life which are bound up with one another.

I/7/5: For, any one of (the three, viz.,) spiritual good, material well-being and sensual pleasures, (if) excessively indulged in, does harm to itself as well as to the other two.

Daily Routine of the King

Kauṭilya prescribes a strict daily routine for the king. The day and night are to be divided into sixteen equal segments, i.e., each segment amounting to one hour and a half. The task of the king for each of these segments are described in the following extracts.

I/19/6: He should divide the day into eight parts as also the night by means of *nālikās*, or by the measure of the shadow (of the gnomon).

I/19/9: Out of them, during the first eighth part of the day, he should listen to measures taken for defence and (accounts of) income and expenditure.

I/19/10: During the second, he should look into the affairs of the citizens and the country people.

I/19/11: During the third, he should take his bath and meals and devote himself to study.

I/19/12: During the fourth, he should receive revenue in cash and assign tasks to heads of departments.

I/19/13: During the fifth, he should consult the council of ministers by sending letters, and acquaint himself with secret information brought in by spies.

I/19/14: During the sixth, he should engage in recreation at his pleasure or hold consultations.

I/19/15: During the seventh, he should review elephants, horses, chariots and troops.

I/19/16: During he eighth, he should deliberate on military plans with the commander-in-chief.

I/19/17: When the day is ended, he should worship the evening twilight.

I/19/18: During the first (eighth) part of the night, he should interview secret agents.

I/19/19: During the second, he should take a bath and meals and engage in study.

I/19/20: During the third, he should go to bed to the strains of musical instruments and sleep during the fourth and the fifth (parts).

I/19/21: During the sixth, he should awaken to the sound of musical instruments and ponder over the teaching of the science (of politics) as well as over the work to be done.

I/19/22: During the seventh, he should sit in consultation (with councillors) and dispatch secret agents.

I/19/23: During the eighth, he should receive blessings from priests, preceptors and chaplain, and see his physician, chief cook and astrologer.

I/19/24: And after going round a cow with her calf and a bull, he should proceed to the assembly hall.

I/19/25: Or, he should divide the day and night into (different) parts in conformity with his capacity and carry out his tasks.

Now, the question arises who is to guide the king and keep him on the path of virtue and rectify him whenever he deviates from the path of virtue because of either his wrong judgment or because of temporary upsurge of evil intentions (Kauṭilya was wise enough to realize that even the most virtuous person may at times be overpowered by the *ṛpus*, i.e., basic vices hidden in the subconscious mind) or bad company. Kauṭilya entrusts this task of guardianship of the king with the *Brāhmaṇa* having proper Vedic learning, who is to be appointed as the Chaplain of the king.

To quote:

I/9/9: He should appoint a Chaplain, who is very exalted in family and character, thoroughly trained in the Veda with its auxiliary sciences, in divine signs, in omens and in the science of politics and capable of counteracting divine and human calamities by means of Atharvan remedies.

I/9/10: And he should follow him as a pupil (does) his teacher, a son his father (or) a servant his master.

I/9/11: *Kṣatriya* power, made to prosper by the *Brāhmaṇa* (Chaplain), sanctified by spells in the form of the counsel of ministers, (and) possessed of arms in the form of compliance with the science (of politics), triumphs, remaining ever unconquered.

Kauṭilya also prescribes for competent and honest ministers, along with the *Brāhmaṇa* Chaplain, as safeguards to keep the king on the path of virtue and propriety as in:

I/7/8: He should set the preceptors or ministers as the bounds of proper conduct (for himself), who should restrain him from occasions of harm, or, when he is erring in private, should prick him with the goad in the form of (the indication of time for the performance of his regular duties by means of) the shadow (of the gnomon) or the *nālikā* (water-clock).

We see from the above analysis that Kauṭilya puts forward the following criteria for a proper ruler (the king) who would bring about prosperity to the country.

(i) The incumbent king should be properly trained in military science, politics, economics, history and tradition of the country, and Vedic *śāstras*.

(ii) He should also have proper education in Ethics, so as to have command over the senses and, thereby, to be free from the basic vices like lust, anger, greed, pride, illusion and jealousy.

(iii) The life of the king should be regulated by tight routine with minimum possible time for rest, sleep and entertainment.

(iv) A Vedic *Brāhmaṇa* (the Chaplain) should regulate the king at all stages of his life.

(v) There should also be a Council of Ministers to advise and regulate the king.

As a matter of fact, Kauṭilya visualized a king (the *Vijīgiṣu*) who would bring about geographical unification of India and make it a strong and prosperous country. In this sense, Kauṭilya's approach was purely normative. Nevertheless, in the real world, there were many such ideal kings. Chandragupta Maurya, the most competent direct disciple of Kauṭilya, was such an ideal king who, for the first time, could bring about political unification of India. His son Vindusāra and grandson Aśoka were also ideal kings. Lack of ideal kings was one of the basic causes of downfall of the Mauryan empire. In the Gupta era and later Indian history till the British rule, prosperity (or downfall) of dynasties was mainly related to the existence (or absence of) ideal kings. In modern democratic India after Independence, the pathetic state of affairs is due mainly to the absence of honest and competent politicians. We shall now discuss this aspect in detail.

As regards the controlling power of the Vedic *Brāhmaṇa* (Chaplain) over the king there is some difference between Manusmṛti and Arthaśāstra of Kauṭilya. The latter assigned more power to the king than prescribed in the earlier texts. This might have become necessary to unify India under a strong king. Whatever be the reason it appears from the prescriptions of the power of the king in Arthaśāstra of Kauṭilya that the Vedic *Brāhmaṇa* appointed by the king himself was not likely to have the same controlling power over the king as his counterpart in Manusmṛti. This may be apprehended from the power Kauṭilya bestows on the king.

To quote:

III/1/38: When all laws are perishing, the king here is the promulgator of laws, by virtue of his guarding the right conduct of the world consisting of the four *varṇas* and four *āśramas*.

III/1/39: A matter in dispute has four feet, law, transaction, custom and the royal edict; (among them) the later one supersedes the earlier one.

III/1/44: He shall decide, with the help of law, a matter in which a settled custom or a matter based on a transaction contradicts the science of law.

III/1/45: When (a text of) the science may be in conflict with any edict in a matter of law, there the edict shall prevail; for, there the written text loses its validity.

The above *ślokas* clearly indicate that Kauṭilya holds royal edict above existing laws, custom and prescriptions of the *śāstras*. So long the king was only the guardian of law and directions of the *śāstras*. Now he becomes a maker of law through royal edicts. Under these circumstances, it is quite unlikely that the Chaplain would have power enough to desist the king from indulging in undesirable activities if the king is adamant to do so. In ancient texts, the king is considered as the wielder of *daṇḍa* (rod of punishment). This concept of *daṇḍa* is not directly associated with our discussion, but knowledge about this concept is likely to give us a deeper insight into the Kingship and the qualities of a perfect king. Now let us pass on to the relevance of the essence of the prescriptions in the two ancient texts for making a competent and honest king.

Relevance for Modern India

Corruption and dishonesty of politicians have become important issues in recent years and, in fact, Indian democratic system has almost become meaningless because of the unethical lifestyles of the politicians of all ranks. The mass media is always replete with news about charges as well as court cases against 'big' politicians. Surprisingly, these corrupt politicians can easily manage to get re-elected and go on pursuing their mischievous activities. Many of them even manage to mobilize overwhelming mass support in spite of their questionable reputation. Otherwise, rigging in elections with the help of hooligans and/or administrative power (in case the party to which the corrupt politicians belong is in power) is the easiest means to get through the 'ballot-battle'.

Immediately after independence, there were only a few corrupt politicians but with the passage of time their number has been increasing continuously. At present, the honest ones have turned out to be an insignificant minority. Moreover, in most of the cases, the corrupt ones are more powerful within the political parties than their honest counterparts. Mischief committed by the powerful politicians includes election-rigging, defalcation of public money, illegal commercial activities, political murders, underhand links and espionage networks with enemy countries, sexual crimes etc. In fact, the democratic system in India has become almost meaningless and the social and political integrity of India has been endangered because of the nefarious activities of these corrupt politicians.

Thus, it is of utmost necessity to investigate the basic cause of this situation and to devise some means to make the politicians free from corruption. Guidelines in Manusmṛti and Arthaśāstra of Kauṭilya may be of considerable help in this regard. Many however argue that these texts had devised guidelines for monarchy and therefore they have no relevance for democratic modern India. But a deeper analysis would reveal that such a viewpoint is completely baseless. In fact, on the basis of the guidelines delineated in these texts for the king (as discussed in detail above), we may also devise similar guidelines for the politicians and political parties in our democratic system. The tentative guidelines may be like this:

(i) There should be strict academic and other essential norms for persons contesting for public posts (the President and the Vice-President of India; the Prime Minister; Chairman and Deputy Chairman of the Rajya Sabha; Speaker and Deputy Speaker of the Lok Sabha; Central Ministers; Governor, Chief Minister and Ministers of each state; MPs; MLAs; Speakers and Deputy Speakers of the State Assemblies; various Representatives of the Municipal Corporations, Municipalities, and the Panchayats etc.).

(ii) Records pertaining to financial matters of all persons holding or contesting for any public position, must be clean.

(iii) No person with criminal records should be permitted to contest any election for a public post.

(iv) The Election Commission and the judicial system must play the role of guardians and regulators of the Public Representatives at all levels.

(v) If any criminal charge against a public representative is proved, he/she should be immediately removed from office and permanently debarred from contesting any election for public office.

(vi) There should be proper measures for providing technical and ethical teachings to persons already holding public office or opting for contesting an election for a public office.

(vii) The judiciary and the election mechanism should be autonomous and independent of the Legislature and administration.

(viii) There should be measures for ensuring honesty, integrity and competence of the judges and the election personnel at all levels.

The most pertinent question in this regard is how far it would be possible for the judicial system and the Election Commission to have controlling power over the politicians since the judges and members of the Election Commission are appointed by the political party in power. So it is quite unlikely that they would have the courage to prevent the politicians in power from indulging in activities harmful for the nation. Such intrepid steps would lead to their immediate dismissal by the ruling party. So we need to look for some alternative solution and here Manusmṛti comes to our help.

Ślokas **7/58** and **7/59** of Manusmṛti (quoted above) entrusts the duty of controlling the king to the Chaplain, a Vedic *Brāhmaṇa*. In a similar fashion in modern India too, we may entrust the task of controlling the politicians in power at different levels to self- sacrificing, greedless and fearless chaplains, who are in essence like *Fakirs* in the modern world. So, our endeavour would be to find out such *Fakir*-like persons and entrust them with the responsibility of controlling the politicians in power at various levels.

12

Globalization

Globalization based on Mobility of both Capital and Labour and Control of Multinational Corporations

The phenomenon of globalization has in recent years become an important issue for debate and discussion. Economists of our country have been polarized into two diametrically opposite camps, one championing globalization and the other opposing it. But if we look into the history of the culture and tradition of ancient India, it would appear that there is no novelty in the concept of globalization. Archaeologists, on the basis of findings of excavations at various parts of the world, have opined that the Indus Valley civilization was closely connected with ancient civilizations of Babylon and Jericho (situated at a place now in modern Israel) around c. 700 B.C. Many opine that the founders of the most dominant aspect of Indian civilization, the Aryans, came from abroad (some region in Central Asia). It is also evident that the so-called Indo-Aryan civilization is a mixture of Aryan and non-Aryan civilizations. This assimilation has endowed unique and lasting characteristics to Indian civilization.

In fact, this assimilated and global feature of Indian civilization was reflected in all aspects of ancient Indian life. The religious texts, mythology, epics, various *śāstras* etc., and the process of their evolution, reflects this continuous process of adoption of new ideas, cultures, ways of life and their assimilation with the old and existing ones. Ancient India had never been a closed-door country. On the contrary, inflow of ideas from abroad had always enriched Indian culture and tradition. The writings of a number of renowned historians and Indologists reveal that various *śāstras* in India (delineating moral codes, ethics, religious rites, legal and administrative procedures, etc.), had assimilated many foreign ideas with the existing ones.

Kauṭilya's Arthaśāstra was largely influenced by Syrian, Greek and Persian ideas. Modern Indian races are an outcome of continuous assimilation of native and immigrating foreign races. Ancient Indian coinage bears the mark of assimilation of Greek and Persian methods of coinage. Indian painting, sculpture, architecture, music and literature had always been enriched by continuous assimilation of foreign ideas and methods (Altekar 1984; Sastri, K.A. Nilakanta, 1967). Studies on early Indian history reveal that India had trade relations with not only Asian countries and Greece, but also with African and European nations (Bose, 1945).

But we should remember that although 'globalization' in the sense of free trade existed in India since the pre-historic time, it was not exactly the process of 'globalization' according to modern terminology, which implies free movement of capital from one country to another without any restrictions. This also indicates freedom of industrial houses owned by foreign nationals to establish branches in any country. These things were completely absent in ancient times. Moreover, in those days, world bodies like the International Monetary Fund (IMF), the World Bank, and the World Trade Organization (WTO), the United Nations Organization (UNO) etc. and modern transport and communication facilities, were totally absent. So we must keep in mind these differences while considering the relevance of ideas embedded in ancient texts in this regard.

Of the ancient texts we have taken up for discussion, Manusmṛti mentions sea voyage only once, which was considered as a mischievous act. But, Kauṭilya's Arthaśāstra attaches much importance to imported commodities and foreign trade, and the countries and places mentioned in various chapters of Arthaśāstra indicate India's wide international connections in those days.

Manusmṛti

3/158: An incendiary, a prisoner, he who eats the food given by the son of an adulteress, a seller of Soma, he who undertakes voyages by sea, a bard, an oil-man, a committer to perjury.

From the above *śloka* it appears that Manu did not look at sea voyage with favour. On the contrary this act was ranked along with mischievous acts like setting fire. The reason may lie in some specific historical conditions.

Arthaśāstra

The following excerpts from Arthaśāstra indicate that foreigners including merchants used to reside in India in those days.

To quote:

II/4/16: In enclosures in the non-residential areas, quarters for guilds and foreign merchants should be situated.

Kauṭilya prescribes that the state should show favour (in terms of tax concessions, higher permissible profit etc.) to the commodities imported from foreign countries; and should take measure to facilitate foreign trade, as is clear from the following *ślokas*.

II/16/11, II/16/12: see Chapter 7 above.

II/16/13: And no law-suit in money matters (should be allowed) against foreign traders, except such as are members (of native concerns) and (their) associates.

But permissible interest rate on loans for foreign trade was higher. This may be because of higher risk involved in foreign trade [see ***ślokas* III/11/1-2** in Chapter 6 of this study].

In Book **II, Chapter 11** of Arthaśāstra (The Examination of Gems to be Entered in the Treasury) Kauṭilya mentions the names of a large number of places from where commodities were brought. Many of these places were situated outside India. This gives an indication of the vast geographical coverage of India's foreign trade in those days.

[see ***ślokas* II/11/2-115** in Chapter 4 of this study].

Many of the places mentioned in these *ślokas* were outside the Maurya Empire but within the geographical boundary of India. But many places like China, Nepal, Suvarṇakuḍḍya, Suvarṇabhūmi, etc., belong to foreign lands. Thus Arthaśāstra gives us an idea of the vast international linkage of India in those days.

One important characteristic of the globalization process in ancient India is that continuous inflow of foreign culture and foreign people never distorted Indian culture and its socio-political and economic systems. Domination only came through direct foreign occupation which, till the tenth century A.D. did not last for a long time. Alexander's invasion could not damage India's culture and tradition at all because his occupation was very short lived. However till the end of British rule considerable damages had been perpetrated on India by forceful imposition of foreign concepts and this was because the globalization of this period was qualitatively different from that which existed till the tenth century. The essential feature of globalization during this period was one of domination by foreigners, whereas during the earlier period it had been one of voluntary assimilation. The millennium long direct foreign domination ended as soon as India achieved independence in 1947, but it still existed in the form of indirect foreign domination through foreign loans and economic dependence on developed nations, especially the USA. This form of indirect domination took a new turn since 1991 when India opted for the globalization according to the dictates of the international bodies like the World Bank, the IMF and the GATT (later on turned into the WTO). Now let us see how our ancient policies regarding globalization are relevant for this new era of globalization.

Relevance for Modern India

In recent years, particularly since the 1990s, globalization has become one of the issues of hot debate. The New Economic Policy adopted in India in 1991, considered globalization as one of its most important objectives and all restrictions on foreign trade are gradually being lifted. As regards this process the economists and other classes of intellectuals of the country have been divided into two major camps – one supporting the process of globalization and the other opposing it. However, it is clear from the discussion of Arthaśāstra and a brief reference to ancient Indian history given above, that ancient India never remained closed to the outside world, and globalization in the wider sense was a common feature of ancient Indian history. Thus, we do not need to be apprehensive of globalization as such; but some aspects of the process of globalization of recent years certainly generate some apprehension. So the question arises how the present form of globalization differs from that of the past and which aspects we should speak against.

It should be made clear that the modern process of global impact on India is a legacy of the colonial domination that started from the emergence of the British rule in India. Till this period all foreign influx into India ultimately resulted in assimilation of foreign culture with the Indian culture, enriching it and generating a composite culture. All domination by foreigners (like that of Alexander's invasion) were only short lived. Most of the foreign invaders ultimately settled in India and became Indians. It cannot be denied that there had been some forceful imposition of foreign culture and ways of life ever since the tenth century A.D. But compared to the British rule their impact was insignificant. The British rule was a qualitatively different thing. It was one of colonial domination. However, since India's political independence, foreign influences have come in the form of inflow of foreign aid and foreign technology. In fact a large part of India's modern industrial development started with foreign aid and foreign technology. In most of the cases, foreign aid was attached with various economic and political strings, revealing the attempts of establishing domination over India by the donor countries. The foreign technology imported was also not assimilated, giving rise to a small modern sector alienated from the rest of the economy of the country since it did not have any spread effect and could not inspire an all round economic development of the country. Still India had some freedom in formulating the policies for her economic development. In fact, contrary to the expectations of the western developed nations India adopted a course of planned economic development and a mixed economy model where the state had a very important role in the economy of the country.

But, the Indian economic system, dominated by the state sector and its regulations on the private sector, came up against serious problems during the 1980s. There were serious problems like industrial recession, hyper inflation, increasing balance of payments deficits etc. Many economists started opining that the concept of mixed economy based on state sector domination was the villain of the piece and India had to make her economy, more market-oriented by ending the 'Quota-Permit Raj'. The success of the so called East Asian tigers gave further impetus for India to liberalize her economy. Various measures towards liberalization had been adopted during the 1980s by the Rajiv Gandhi government and these had produced some beneficial results, especially, in overcoming the industrial recession but even this partial liberalization could not help Indian economy come out of the basic problems it had been inflicted with. The condition was most serious in case of balance of payments. The magnitude of deficits in balance of payments went on increasing rapidly. The protagonists of liberalization opined that complete liberalization was the only way out. This was also the advice of the world bodies like the World Bank and the IMF.

The immediate cause that prompted the government of India to make a complete policy change was the precarious foreign exchange reserves (only Rs. 2,400 crore) in June 1991, which would meet import requirements of only three weeks. Moreover, as international agencies lowered India's credit rating, a run on foreign deposits in India was apprehended. The only way out was a complete change of policy and thorough structural reforms which included globalization of the economy by gradually removing all quota restrictions on imports and reduction of tariffs to the minimum possible level. India also had to devalue the Rupee substantially in two installments. Various restrictions, for example provisions under the Foreign Exchange Regulations Act, 1973, Monopolies and Restrictive Trade Practices Act, 1969 etc. had to be removed to provide free access to Indian economy to the giant multinational corporations of the developed nations. In fact, many of these measures had been indirectly imposed on India by the world bodies, most of which were controlled by the USA. When the World Trade Organization (WTO) was set up in January 1995, India became one of its founder members and vowed to abide by its guidelines regarding integrating Indian economy with the international market.

More than a decade and a half have elapsed since the adoption of the policy of globalization and now it is apprehended by many that with further opening up of the economy, India will come under the direct domination of the giant multinational corporations, over which the Government of India has no control (Dhingra, op.cit.: 543-92). From practical experience it appears that the apprehension is not at all unfounded. India in recent years has been confronted with many adverse consequences, many of which may be attributed to globalization. The growth rates of per capita national income, industry and agriculture, have been far from satisfactory. The failure has been most prominent in the field of agriculture. The salutary effects of the so called Green Revolution have almost died down and it has been realized that further breakthrough in Indian agriculture is not possible without thorough land reforms, which is not likely to be compatible with the process of globalization as undertaken by India at the behest of the world bodies.

One of the most serious problems arising out of the process of globalization is the rapid aggravation in the employment situation. All available data indicate that in course of globalization in India, the employment situation has considerably deteriorated. The annual rate of growth of employment in the organized sector in India declined from 1.4 per cent in 1991 to – 6 per cent in 2001 (*Statistical Outline of India* 2003-04; 166). All evidences reveal that there is a stagnation of the unorganized industrial sector, and the agricultural sector is already overburdened. So, the ranks of open, and disguised unemployment and under- employment have been swelling continuously with serious socio-economic consequences. It is also justifiably apprehended that rapid inflow of international speculative capital in course of globalization has made the Indian economy more volatile and subject to the whims of the international speculators.

Another alarming point is that the WTO is serving the interests of the MNCs of the developed nations at the cost of the LDCs (less development countries) like India. The actual experience of these countries since the establishment of the WTO has been quite disappointing. For example, globalization of trade in agriculture has benefited mainly the multinational trading companies of the DCs (developed countries) in agricultural commodities (mainly of the USA). This view was rightly aired by all the LDC members of the WTO in the Seattle Conference of the WTO. They expressed similar grievances in the subsequent conferences of the organization.

Thus in brief we can say that the process of global influence in ancient India was one of assimilation of global ideas whereas now it is one of domination by the international business interests. Manu may have spoken against global influences because he had similar apprehension of domination by foreigners.

To conclude it may be said that the lessons from ancient texts regarding globalization is that we should welcome the process, but after preserving our sovereignty and freedom (economic, political, strategic, social and cultural). The most important matter in this context is related to inter-country free movement of capital. The most crucial among all the conditions imposed by the world bodies on countries undergoing structural reforms and globalization is the provision for free inflow of foreign capital. At the same time there is hardly any provision for free international mobility of labour. According to the General Agreement on Trade Related Services (GATS), there should be free international movement of both capital and labour relating to the service sector. On the basis of this agreement, all the LDCs including India have given free access to capital of the developed countries in their service sector. For example India has permitted foreign banks and insurance companies to operate here but the developed countries have restricted the inflow of unskilled labour from the LDCs into their countries under various pretexts. So, the excess capital of the developed countries are getting the opportunity to be invested in the markets of the LDCs, depressing the rates of interest in these countries. But the LDCs are not getting any facility to reduce the burden of surplus labour.

Thus the entire process is one-sided, benefiting the capital-surplus developed countries, while labour-surplus less developed countries are losing. So the first and foremost thing for making the process of globalization harmless for India is to create provision for free international movement of labour. To this end, a combined effort of all the Third World countries is an urgent necessity. If free movement of labour is not possible, India and for that matter, all the developing countries should try their best to resist the free inflow of capital from the developed countries, particularly the speculative ones and those that try to establish domination of the MNCs over their economies.

References

Altekar, A.S. (1984): *State and Government in Ancient India*, Motilal Banarasidass, Delhi.

Bose, A. (1945): *Social and Rural Economy of Northern India*, Calcutta University.

Sastri, K.A.Nilakanta (ed.) (1967): *Age of the Nandas and Mauryas*, Motilal Banarasidass, Delhi.

Statistical Outline of India 2003-2004, Tata Services Limited, Mumbai.

Index